ENCOUNTER
THROUGH THE
BIBLE

GENESIS | EXODUS | LEVITICUS

Copyright © Scripture Union 2011
First published 2011
ISBN 978 1 84427 574 8

Scripture Union England and Wales
207–209 Queensway, Bletchley, Milton Keynes MK2 2EB, UK
Email: info@scriptureunion.org.uk
Website: www.scriptureunion.org.uk

Scripture Union Australia
Locked Bag 2, Central Coast Business Centre, NSW 2252
Website: www.su.org.au

Scripture Union USA
PO Box 987, Valley Forge, PA 19482
Website: www.scriptureunion.org

The daily devotional notes for *Encounter through the Bible* have previously appeared in *Encounter with God*, a Scripture Union dated daily Bible guide. Supplementary material written especially for this volume by John Grayston.

The introductory material is adapted for this series from *The Bible in Outline* (Scripture Union, 1985) and *Explorer's Guide to the Bible* (John Grayston, Scripture Union, 2008).

British Library Cataloguing-in-Publication Data: a catalogue record of this book is available from the British Library.

Series editor: 'Tricia Williams
Printed and bound in India by Nutech Print Services
Cover design by Heather Knight

Scripture Union is an international Christian charity working with churches in more than 130 countries, providing resources to bring the good news about Jesus to children, young people and families and to encourage them to develop spiritually through the Bible and prayer. As well as co-ordinating a network of volunteers, staff and associates who run holidays, church-based events and school groups, we produce a wide range of publications and support those who use our resources through training programmes.

CONTENTS

MEETING GOD

For many years Christians throughout the world have found the 'Scripture Union method' a tremendous help in deepening their relationship with God as they read the Bible. Here is a modern version of that method, which aims to help you to make your time with God a true meeting with him. You may like to refer to it each day as a supplement to the comments in this volume.

COME TO GOD as you are. Worship him for his power, greatness and majesty. Bring him your feelings and needs. Ask for his Holy Spirit to help you understand and respond to what you read.

READ the Bible passage slowly and thoughtfully, listening out for what God is saying to you.

TALK WITH GOD about what you have read. These suggestions may help you:

- 'Lord, thank you for your Word to me today. What special message are you shouting out to me, or whispering to me, in these verses?'

- 'Lord, I want to meet you here; tell me more about yourself, Father, Son and Holy Spirit, in these verses.'

- 'I don't know what today holds for me, Lord. I need your guidance, your advice. I need you to help me be alert. Direct my heart and thoughts to those words you know I need.'

- 'Lord, your Word is a mirror in which I often find myself. Show me myself here, as you see me, alone or with others. Thank you that you understand how I feel as I read your Word.'

- 'Lord, there are things here I don't understand. Please help me through the notes in this guide, or give me others who may help me.'

RESPOND Try to find a key thought or phrase which has come to you from this passage to carry with you through the day. Pray for people who are on your mind at the moment. Determine to share your experiences with others.

USING THIS GUIDE

Encounter through the Bible is a devotional Bible guide that can be used any time. It uses some of the best of the *Encounter with God* Bible series to guide the reader through whole Bible books in a systematic way. Like *Encounter with God*, it is designed for thinking Christians who want to interpret and apply the Bible in a way that is relevant to the problems and issues of today's world.

It is hoped that eventually the series will lead readers through the whole Bible. This volume covers Genesis, Exodus and Leviticus. Look out for the other guides available now:

Old Testament
Numbers, Deuteronomy, Joshua
Judges, Ruth, 1 & 2 Samuel

New Testament
Matthew, Mark
Luke, John

The notes are arranged in Bible book order – in this volume, Genesis to Leviticus. Each Bible book series begins with an introduction giving an overview of the book and its message. These aim to help you to get a grip on the book as a whole.

Each daily note begins with a call to worship which should help you consciously to come into God's presence before you read the passage. The main 'explore' section aims to bring out the riches hidden in the text. The response section at the end of the note may include prayer or praise and suggest ways of applying the message to daily living.

GENESIS

The rest of the Bible would make very little sense but for the book of Genesis. It answers the 'big' questions, such as: why are we here and where did we come from? Genesis speaks of the beginning of the world, of human beings and society, of families and of nations, of sin and salvation. In particular, it speaks of the start of the Hebrew race, telling the foundational stories of Abraham, Isaac and Jacob. The story of Joseph prepares us for the next great chapter of God's story: the Exodus.

Genesis is the first book of the 'Pentateuch' – the five 'books of the Law'. Although we can't know for certain who actually wrote these, the New Testament implies that Moses was the author – and it is reasonable to see Moses as an editor who put together stories and facts, some of which would have already have been in wide circulation before his time.

Genesis sets the scene for the rest of the Bible: God made the world; human disobedience and its consequences have spoilt it; God has a plan to put things right. And, even here, in this first book of the Bible, there are hints of the coming Saviour (Genesis 3:15).

Outline

1 The story of creation	1,2
2 The story of mankind	3:1 – 11:30
2 The story of Abraham	11:31 – 25:18
3 The story of Isaac	25:19 – 27:40
4 The story of Jacob	27:41 – 37:1
5 The story of Joseph	37:2 – 50:26

GOD AT WORK

Pray that God will enable you to see this well-known passage with fresh eyes.

Since the second century AD some Christian commentators have seen the creation account in Genesis 1 as an extended metaphor, picturing God as a worker doing a week's work. Of course there is a sense in which God's work is unique. Only God can truly 'create' things. The Hebrew verb used for 'create' is only ever used in the Old Testament with God as the active subject, and there is never any mention of the material out of which God creates things. This is one basis of the Christian doctrine that God created the universe 'from things that are not visible'.[1] The use of the verb in verse 20 of the great sea monsters is a response to pagan ideas about the creator having to do battle with the monsters of chaos before being able to create the world. Israel's God created any monsters that exist, and did not have to battle with them in order to form the earth!

Elsewhere in the story the verb 'to make' is used. It is used in Hebrew for any artisan at work. God's work is depicted as planned and carried out in an orderly way. When initially created the world was 'formless' and 'empty'. God spends three days forming or shaping it by acts of 'separation', producing three 'shaped' areas. Three more days are then spent filling each area with appropriate creatures. As a result day one corresponds to day four, and so on (with two acts of creation on each day). Every evening God was pleased with his work, saying 'that was a good day's work'. The outcome was the perfect execution of a wonderful creative concept – our earth. In all this, God sets an example of what it means to be good workers in his world.

'Lord, help me to do a good day's work for you, following your own example of ordered, purposeful creative effort.'

---

[1] Heb 11:3, NRSV

IMAGING GOD

Lord, teach me not to try to 'play god', but truly to 'image' you by my character and my behaviour.

GENESIS 1:24 – 2:4A

The climax of God's work was the creation of human beings. This is marked by a 'pause for thought' as God deliberates before acting (v 26a), showing that this is a carefully thought-out action. Then the verb 'to create' is used three times (v 27). All this emphasises that humans are special. Alone of all the creatures, we are created 'in the image of God'. What does this mean? Two things seem clear. First, it refers to the whole human person, not just one aspect or attribute. We are to 'image' God in every part of our personality and life. Secondly, in the ancient Near East images of rulers were set up to show people who ruled them. Humans are God's representatives on earth. In fact he commands us to rule it in this capacity. Seen in this light, the command not to make any graven image of God[1] takes on new meaning. Such images not only dishonour God, they demean humans. Idolatry leads to human sacrifice – either literally or by 'sacrificing' people to the achievement of some end.

We are to 'image' God as we do the work he has given us – ruling his creation. Among other things this means not exploiting it selfishly but using it in ecologically sound ways. We will 'image' God in our work if we reflect God's characteristics – love, justice, wisdom and so on. To do this we must be living close to God. That is why day seven of the creation week is important. A day of rest from our normal work is good for our bodies and minds, but it also helps us avoid making our work an idol and gives us the time and opportunity to get to know God better.

'So whether you eat or drink or whatever you do, do it all for the glory of God'.[2] Is there any task you can more consciously do to glorify God?

---

[1] Exod 20:4,5 [2] 1 Cor 10:31

WORK AND WORSHIP

What does 'worship' mean for you? When do you do it?

Having given an overall view of creation, the story now homes in on the creation of human beings. The special nature of humans is brought out by the fact that having 'formed a man from the dust of the ground' (v 7), as God does the animals (v 19), he then breathes into him 'the breath of life'. The man is put in the garden 'to work it and take care of it' (v 15). Work was part of God's original intention for us. The garden was not meant as a playground for pampered pets, but as a training ground for God's co-workers.

The verbs used in verse 15 for 'to work' and 'to take care of' are the same verbs that are used in the Old Testament for what the priests do in the tabernacle and Temple. Caring for God's garden is as much worship as what goes on in the sanctuary. What we do for six days of the week is simply a different form of worship from that which happens on the seventh day. That, at least, is how God wants us to see it.

After being told several times that God saw his work as 'good', and once 'very good', it ought to come as a shock to us to find God saying 'it is not good' (v 18). What was not good was that the man had no one to work alongside him. The word used for 'helper' is most often used of God helping Israel, so it does not imply any inferiority. In naming the animals the man realises none can meet his need. When he names the woman he recognises her as his true partner.

What difference would it make to your attitude to work and the way you do it today if you saw it as worshipping God?

WORK IN A FALLEN WORLD

What makes your work frustrating? Pray that as you consider this passage God will show you something to do about it.

GENESIS 3

The serpent got Adam and Eve to feel dissatisfied with being God's workers, and wanting to be their own bosses. So they disobeyed God and ate of the forbidden fruit. At first the serpent seemed to be vindicated. Despite God's threat (2:17) they did not die immediately, at least not physically. This, however, points to the fact that in the Bible death is wider than physical mortality. It is being out of relationship with God, the source of all life. So, when Moses offers the Israelites a covenant relationship with God he offers them a choice between life and death.[1]

This story does not give us an answer to the question of the ultimate origin of evil. It is important to note that the serpent was a creature (v 2), not another god. As a creature the serpent is ultimately under God's control. What the story does give us is an important insight into many of our problems. As soon as Adam and Eve sinned they died in the sense that their relationship with God was broken. They now hid from him in fear instead of enjoying his presence. From this broken relationship flow our psychological problems (they were each uncomfortable with themselves), our social problems (Adam blamed Eve, and their relationship became marked by conflict, v 16b), and our ecological problems (the ground was cursed, v 17b). In particular, work became toilsome. God's purpose in Christ is to restore harmony in his damaged creation.[2] The new creation is pictured as a place where work is again free of frustration.[3] Since Christ has brought in the new creation[4] we should be seeking to make it a reality in our workplaces.

Think about your workplace. Pray about the problems in it and see if God shows you any practical steps that might be taken to deal with them.

---

[1] Deut 30:15 [2] Col 1:20 [3] Isa 65:21–23 [4] 2 Cor 5:17

GRACE OUTSIDE EDEN

Despite our worst efforts God can achieve good through us. Thank him today.

What makes Cain's sin particularly heinous is that it was not just murder, it was fratricide. He killed his brother. Note how this is driven home by the repeated use of the word 'brother' in verses 8-11. There is a sense in which, as co-workers bearing the image of God, all humans are 'family'. For that reason we cannot deny responsibility for another's welfare, as Cain tried to with regard to Abel's.

God punished Cain for his sin, but tempered this with mercy. The mark did not remove the anguish of homelessness, but it did remove the fear of being murdered. Banished from God's garden, Cain built a city. This might seem an inauspicious start for human culture - it has been largely in cities that godless culture has developed. Yet God took the city and wove it into his purposes. Jerusalem, originally a pagan city, became Zion, 'the city of our God'.[1] John's vision of the new heaven and earth centres on the new Jerusalem, a city into which the nations bring their glory and honour.[2] God will take up the good fruits of human labour and incorporate them into his new creation. This is God's 'common grace' at work. It is in Cain's line that important developments in human culture take place - domestication of animals, music and metalworking (vs 20-22). Of course each of these can be used for either good or ill. This is why the other development reported in this chapter is vitally important - 'At that time people began to call on the name of the LORD' (v 26). Used in the context of work as worship of the Lord, technology can be a boon. Used simply to achieve our own selfish ends, it often becomes a bane.

The results of your work could have a place in the new Jerusalem – just think of that as you do it today!

---

[1] Ps 48:1 [2] Rev 21:26

HOPE IN A FALLEN WORLD

It may be just a list of names to us, but God knew them each individually. Thank God that he knows and loves you.

GENESIS 5

Long genealogies are not a familiar part of modern Western literature, but are quite common in some cultures. In the Bible they are sometimes an important part of the 'storyline'. It may be unwise to try to use them for chronological purposes. In other ancient Near Eastern genealogies, such as the Sumerian 'King Lists' which have similarities to the genealogies in Genesis, numbers seem to be used more for symbolism than chronology. The genealogy in Genesis 5 carries the storyline of Genesis forward from the Garden of Eden to the flood. It makes a number of important points.

First, it makes clear that despite the sin of Adam and Eve in the garden, humans are still made in the image of God. Genesis 9:6 shows that this is the right way to understand verse 3.[1] The fall has, however, affected our ability to 'image' God. Paul speaks of the image being restored to us in Christ.[2] However, if we had lost it altogether, we would be no different from the animals. Secondly, the creation blessing is still operative. The genealogy itself is testimony to it since it is evidence of the human race 'multiplying'. Yet the effect of God's judgement is seen in the repeated phrase 'and then he died'. There are two beacons of hope. The fellowship with God that Adam and Eve enjoyed in the garden is still possible. Enoch 'walked … with God'. Moreover, his fellowship with God transcended death (v 24a)– one of the effects of the fall.

Noah provides a more down-to-earth prospect. His skill in growing vines (9:20) brought relief from another effect of the fall, the toil that now accompanies work.

Think of people who are beacons of hope for you. Thank God for them and pray for them. Could you be one for someone?

---

[1] *See also* James 3:9 [2] Rom 8:29

AGAINST GRAVITY

God is bringing the world to its fulfilment. 'Lord, open our eyes as we look for your coming among us today.'

'Obedience to gravity is the greatest sin.' Simone Weil's words express the choice before each of us: to commit to the living God, or to let go and yield to the gravitational pull of an unbelieving world.[1] Noah felt 'gravity' as the demonic in human society, evoked in strange images (vs 1-4), as blasphemous genetic mutations (v 2) and half-caste gods, Nephilim, pursuing their titanic predatory lusts (v 4). It conjures up a nightmare vision of rebel-man, the rampant God-hater, in his arrogant drive for the superhuman.[2] The demonic is not necessarily spectacular in its manifestations; it seeps through also in everyday attitudes. Jesus pictured 'the days of Noah' as a complacent, apathetic, self-engrossed and frivolous society who ridiculed attention to God's call.[3] Does that sound familiar? Such an overwhelming consensus exerts a tremendous pull on a believing minority. Noah's sustained obedience is incredible. How did he do it? How was it that God's call came with such conviction and power in his mind, enough to defy gravity by doing 'everything just as God commanded him' (v 22), responding in practical obedience to 'things not yet seen'?[4] The explanation is, 'he walked ... with God' (v 9). But if that phrase conjures up a vision of an unearthly mystic with recourse to secret springs of spiritual power, we should remember that obeying God is an act of communion with him. In the act of cutting wood and hammering nails for the ark Noah was walking with God. With every lick of paint he overcame the greatest sin, obedience to gravity. The call of God will grow in conviction and clarity in our hearts as we do it.[5]

Receive the work before you this day as your opportunity for communion with God, to walk and to build with him. 'We are priests in our own tasks, in our everyday work' (Martin Luther).

[1] Rom 12:1,2   [2] Gen 3:5   [3] Matt 24:37,38   [4] Heb 11:7   [5] John 8:31,32

RE-CREATION

The ark, like the cross, is the sign that God rules in history. Pray to live in the joy of that reality.

GENESIS 7

The world is always God's world. He handles creation like a potter who refuses to abandon the collapsed clay on his wheel, but ceaselessly works upon it until he brings it through to completion.[1] That holds true at the cosmic and the personal level. God is not, first, a creator and only then a saviour. And creation is not a fixed or rigid construct, for God is moment-by-moment bringing it into being. He saves by re-creating. Not only at the end of time but in present history he is 'making everything new'[2] as he takes hold of evil, death and chaos to bring out good, life and order.

The flood was a severe act of 'redemptive re-creation', a breaking and remaking, a death and resurrection, and at unimaginable cost to God. He was on the inside with his rebellious children. Consider these two things: first, the divine grief and pain (6:6); secondly, when God blessed Adam he imparted something of his own life into man (1:28), for that is the biblical meaning of blessing. Therefore, when the waters of judgement closed over the head of sinful man, the divine presence in man was engulfed in judgement also; a pre-figure of what was to happen in Christ at the cross.[3] The ark, however, rode above the waters of destruction (v 17).[4] The animals were saved because they followed Noah who obeyed God. Noah led the creatures to safety. In that sense they took man for their example, trusting him for their welfare. It is Noah's care for his creatures, not our present exploitation and maltreatment of them, which honours man's stewardship of nature (1:26).

The ark had no rudder. What faith! Are you prepared to allow God to lead you, even when you do not know where you are going?[5]

---

[1] Jer 18:1–10 [2] Rev 21:5 [3] Isa 53:1–9 [4] Rom 8:18–25 [5] Heb 11:8

THE REMEMBERING

The astonishing ark enterprise was possible because one man knew how to rest in God's faithful love. Lord, teach me this secret.

GENESIS 8

How fascinating that a man whose exploits saw time divided in two (antediluvian and post-deluvian) should be named Noah. It means 'rest'. The Scriptures 'testify to the fact that man's rest is a treasure and capacity which is not a matter of course but is deeply bound up with trust in the Lord' (H Wolff). Far from condoning detachment, look what it did for Noah. He found his rest in the fact that 'God *remembered*' him (v 1, my italics), a rich word meaning that God brought Noah to the forefront of his mind and held him there.[1] A resolution: I will start each day by remembering the God who is forever remembering me.[2] This attunes heart and mind to the Holy Spirit and puts the day's activity in perspective.

God's remembering is potent and creative, it makes things happen and drives the divine purposes forward through history. 'The waters flooded ... but God remembered Noah' (7:24; 8:1). Yet there is a tension, one which Noah dramatises graphically: salvation came *slowly*, 150 days on those desolating waters (vs 6-16). We know the feeling for we too 'wait eagerly...'.[3] Noah lived by faith and not by the appearance of things which were utterly depressing. But he was given his signs and evidence - clearing skies, receding water, the dove's olive sprig - how else could he have known God was remembering him? We, too, should look for and receive the Holy Spirit's activity in us as seal, deposit and guarantee of the Father's remembering.[4] And in the Spirit to be assured that our Lord holds us in the forefront of his mind, steady within his gaze whose every glance heals and saves.

Consciously bring every aspect of your life, and particularly things which terrify, into the sphere of God's remembering, and rest there.

---

[1] Isa 49:15 [2] Deut 7:18; 24:9 [3] Rom 8:23 [4] 2 Cor 1:21,22

UNDER THE RAINBOW

Whenever the rainbow appears in the clouds... Lord, help me to remember your promises.

GENESIS 9:1-17

After the flood the world still witnesses to the Creator: 'the world is charged with the grandeur of God ... The birds sing to him, the thunder speaks of his terror, the lion is like his strength, the sea is like his greatness, the honey like his sweetness; they are something like him, they make him known, they tell of him, they give him glory'.[1] But we detect a change of mood, a new realism about humanity, the paradox that the only beings to bear the image of God menace creation with their violence (4:24; 6:11).[2] Creation, and not least people themselves, must be protected against such destructive energies (v 6). Humans are reaffirmed in their dominion over nature (vs 2,3) but made accountable to God who is at the root of all life, thus making life of every kind holy. Hence the sanctity of the blood (vs 4,5). Our relationship with nature is therefore inescapably a moral one, for we handle God's holy property, and should exercise the privilege of control with conscience and compassion.[3]

In a passage essential to a Christian's thinking about the great 'life' issues of abortion, euthanasia, capital punishment and suicide (vs 4-6), three times God warns, 'I will demand an accounting' (v 5). Although we must constantly be vigilant against tendencies of governments to plunder and pollute creation, its continuance to the end of time does *not* depend upon us.[4] God has covenanted - unilaterally, unconditionally, and forever - to sustain creation (vs 8-17). Man can no more tamper with that destiny than he can with the rainbow in the sky (v 16).

Look around your home. Look at your lifestyle. Are you handling creation 'with care'?

---

[1] Gerard Manley Hopkins, 1844–89 [2] Rom 3:9–18 [3] Ezek 33:25 [4] Rev 21:1–6

LIVING THE EXPERIMENT

The Lord forms his image in people through their experiences in the real world. Christians should be the most real of people.

GENESIS 9:18–29

Noah's first act in the new world was to worship (8:20); his second was to experiment (9:20). A thankful, exploring approach to the world is a richly satisfying way to live; it is the experimentation of faith.[1] Noah's saving faith on the ark did not save him from risks involved in living experimentally on land. Believers understand this since they chance everything on the promises of God. We put our full weight on them and see what happens. Jesus qualified as our Saviour only because he too lived in the experiment of faith.[2] Therefore we reject all myths of a trouble-free existence in this world. We know a better way, a more real way, which is to trust in 'the Lord of the experiment'. He allows us to live our lives in the real world, this beautiful but dangerous world, while persuading the whole flux of experience to work 'for the good of those who love him'.[3]

Noah found that yes, wine gladdens human hearts[4] but also that a drugged mind is dangerously (and sexually) vulnerable. As for the salacious son (vs 20–22,24), Ham's tendencies passed into the Canaanite cultural bloodstream (v 18) to emerge in the institutionalised gross immoralities of Baal-worship which used sex as a way of controlling the powers of nature. In our own culture sex is exploited as a potent means of self-expression. Whenever sex is used as a means to an end it splits the image of God as found in the *whole* woman and the *whole* man within their commitment of binding love.[5] 'Radical experimenters will dare to opt for sexual purity.[6]

Reflect on what you are learning experimentally, in your exploration of life. Are you making your hard-won wisdom available to others?

---

[1] Ps 111:1–10 [2] Heb 2:10–18 [3] Rom 8:28 [4] Ps 104:15 [5] Gen 1:27 [6] 1 Cor 6:12–19; 2 Cor 6:14 – 7:1

AMONG THE NATIONS

God's purposes drive on in the movements of peoples and nations.
Lord, awaken us to your saving presence in the world.

GENESIS 10

God is not the puppeteer of nations, but allows them their freedom,
while drawing all things to serve his purposes. World news is news
of God: 'the nations' are the theatre of his activity and vehicle of his
purposes.[1] Grasping the significance of this, we attend to world news
more carefully and prayerfully. We become habitual world-watchers
– more globally minded. 'Reading the morning papers becomes a
religious act, for it sets the agenda of what must be repaired this day'
(Kushner).[2] But if world affairs do not affect our thinking and praying
we imply God's absence, or his powerlessness, or that salvation is
essentially a 'spiritual' programme floating above the messy rough
and tumble of 'the nations'. In which case the gospel would be little
more than a personal therapy alongside many other therapies. But
God's primal covenant with Noah was an unconditional and universal
promise of blessing for the whole human family and its world-home,
nature.[3] It was a promise carried forward in the journeys of the
Japheth-peoples into Asia Minor (vs 2–4); the Ham-peoples south
towards Egypt (vs 6–20) and the Shem-nations into the region of Israel
(vs 21–31).

These are not sociological abstractions called 'humanity' or
'society', nor are they merely swarms of individuals. They are people-
groups living within complex webs of integrated relationships –
cultural, linguistic and political – in the spiritual, personal, material
and social spheres. That Jesus became the man he was, living
within such a people as one of them and then ministering his words
and works along the pathways of their web of relationships, must
illuminate our own outreach and faith-sharing today.[4] For most
people, belonging *precedes* believing.

**How shall we pray for the world? That our Lord will 'see of the travail of
his soul and ... be satisfied'.[5]**

[1] Isa 2:2–5 [2] Luke 12:54–56 [3] Acts 17:24–29 [4] Matt 13:53–57 [5] Isa 53:11,
AV

THE TOWER OF CONFUSION

Where civilisation builds itself up against God, expect the spirit of Babel.
Lord, glorify your name in the city.

GENESIS 11:1–9

Sin's great trick is to create in our minds an illusion of autonomy from God.[1] The icon of this earth-dream is the city. The prototype for Babel was in the first post-Eden city, which Cain built to protect himself from God's protection (4:8–17). Next, at Babel men set out to 'make a name for ourselves' (v 4), not in our use of the term, meaning to build a reputation, but in the biblical sense of 'he who names is Lord'.[2] As long as God does the naming, the defining and appointing of one's meaning, purpose and place then, like it or not, we belong to God. But sinful man doesn't like it a bit. He builds his city both as the symbol of his self-sufficiency and as the means of its achievement, for with all the benefits of urban technology – frankly, who needs God (v 3)? So runs the myth of Babel, of Rome, of New York and the 'megalopolis' of our era. 'It is only in an urban civilisation that man has the metaphysical possibility of saying "I killed God"' (Jacques Ellul). Or harnessed God – for he has his uses.

A tower connects city to heaven from where the deity exercises a chaplaincy role. He sanctions schemes and rubber-stamps decisions, imparting a spiritual glow to our God-rejecting autonomy. But God will not stay up there on his tower; he says, 'Come, let us go down' (v 7). The city-myth carries within it the ticking bomb of its own failure: unrootedness, unbridled restlessness, disunity, confusions between people (vs 7,8). Yet the city remains the ideal. Its transformation from Babel-Babylon to Jerusalem, the city of God, is the final picture of creation.[3]

Consider Abraham. He 'made his home' where God had placed him yet 'was looking forward to the city with foundations, whose architect and builder is God.'[4] Pray for that balance.

---

[1] Ps 14:1–4 [2] Gen 2:19,20 [3] Rev 21:1–5; 22:1–6 [4] Heb 11:8–10

AFTER BABEL

God reaches the many through the few. The quality, not the quantity of his 'few' is crucial. Lord, make us faithful witnesses.

GENESIS 11:10–32

Election is not everyone's favourite doctrine. It smacks of elitism. But election is at the heart of God's way of mission.[1] Always the divine perspective is universal and cosmic,[2] but his plan unfolds through individuals. Out of the catastrophe of the flood, one man, Noah, is called. From the hopelessness of Babel, one couple is chosen to carry forward the plan for all humankind, Abram and Sarai (v 31). The biblical story therefore swings between the vast panorama of cosmic purposes, and the focused-down details of particular individuals and small groups.[3] But why? Why doesn't God Almighty reveal himself simultaneously to millions as effectively as he does to individuals? Why not sweep whole populations into the kingdom, in the power of the irresistible Holy Spirit, since that is what he does when he calls the few? For an answer we must contemplate the nature of God himself. He is not Allah, a solitary monad, but three persons related in the unity of love. Thus his image in 'Adam' is man-and-woman in relationship.

The ultimate vision of restored humanity is of city life teeming with people living together. God's way with the world involves people going to people: 'neighbour' is at the heart of authentic mission, 'This means that the gift of salvation is bound up with openness to one another' (Lesslie Newbigin). Everywhere God calls his people into existence through faith in Christ. They are not a club of favoured people, the exclusive beneficiaries of covenant blessings, they are rather its witnesses, its agents, holding the gospel on behalf of the world; 'neighbours' who take the word of life to others; called for service not privilege. It is a tough calling.[4]

In contrast to our almost neurotic preoccupation with the size of congregations, the New Testament makes virtually no reference to numbers. Election means, 'stop counting and start weighing'.

---

[1] 1 Pet 2:9,10 [2] Col 1:15–19 [3] Eph 1:3–14 [4] 2 Cor 5:18–20

TRAVELS: AROUND AND OUT

'O LORD ... You know everything I do ... You go before me and follow me
... I can never get away from your presence!'[1]

GENESIS 12

Leaving home and homeland is always challenging. New culture, new language, new people, new tasks, new insects and many new situations must all be faced. Today it is perhaps much easier; information about the new land is freely available and travel is not difficult. I am shortly to visit home for the second time after only a year in Africa, and I know that in two or three years I will leave here for good. But for Abraham and Sarah it was different. Responding to God's call meant they would never see their country or their family again. They responded anyway, even though they realised that their only point of stability in the new land would be their relationship with the God that they were just beginning to know. Would that be enough? This passage raises a number of issues relating to that question.

Once in the land, they travelled around and at each place they stopped, Abraham built an altar, affirming his understanding that God remained with him and that in this land God would be worshipped – by his family at least. We often think of Abraham as in constant contact with God, holding regular conversations, but that is not how the story is told. Many times, sometimes for years, Abraham and Sarah were left to work it all out for themselves. When famine came, apparently God's presence with them in the land was no longer enough and they decided to leave. They went to Egypt to find food and also found trouble! They eventually went back under armed escort. Maybe God's knowledge that their desire really was to follow him caused him to ensure their return to the land of his promised presence. It is encouraging to realise that unwise decisions do not automatically mean the end of a previously accepted calling.

Many Christians have, through war or disaster, lost everything – home, family, money, health. Only God is left. The challenge is clear: for me, would that really be enough?

1 Ps 139:1,3,5,7, NLT

DECISIONS, DECISIONS

'Choose for yourselves this day whom you will serve ... But as for me and my household, we will serve the LORD.'[1]

GENESIS 13

Had Lot been adopted by Abraham as an orphan or was he part of the wider family that Abraham had been told to leave behind in Ur? Their property being kept separate could imply the latter. Although the issue is not explicitly raised, Abraham's decision to take Lot with them had wide and not always positive consequences. Here, however, we are faced with another decision. The extent of their joint property was causing problems. Abraham's insight that separation was better than quarrelling is perhaps relevant to similar power struggles in today's world!

Lot is given the choice. He is often criticised for taking it but in some cultures even today if an elder offers the choice it would be offensive not to accept graciously. Abraham would be praised for offering the choice but Lot not condemned for accepting! Lot's choice, however, was based on materialistic grounds: what looked the better land. (Frequently for us, too, considerations of economic prosperity can, wrongly, become paramount.) We are then told, almost as a postscript, that the people of that area were 'extremely wicked' (v 13, NLT). The way it is added seems to be stressing that this had not affected Lot's choice one way or the other.

Chapter 19 will raise the question as to whether it should have done! Once Lot has gone, God makes it clear to Abraham that Lot's choice was completely irrelevant. The land, everything he could see in every direction, *including* the land that Lot chose, would be given to Abraham's family. Is it significant that it was only after Lot had left that God expands his promise so that the whole land will belong to Abraham and his descendants? Abraham responds by moving on and building another altar. What counted for him was that God was still present.

Think about these issues. On what grounds do I base my choices? What am I taking with me that it might be better to be separated from?

[1] Josh 24:15

SHARING THE SPOILS

'We must help the weak, remembering the words the Lord Jesus himself said: "It is more blessed to give than to receive."'[1]

Although his evident expertise (vs 14-16) suggests that Abraham may have had previous military experience, we have no indication that he had any great desire to be a soldier! It was certainly not part of his calling. But even though Lot was now separated, it was Abraham who had brought him here and family responsibilities are significant. Immediately he heard about Lot's capture Abraham had no question: something had to be done and he had to do it. It would be nice to think that Christians today would respond as quickly to the needs of suffering brothers and sisters separated by culture and geography, and as quickly recognise responsibility for action. Sometimes circumstances, needs and cultural constraints do mean we have to take on roles we have no desire to undertake and for which we feel no particular call. There is no mention of God in these early verses but the later ones are very clear that it was God who enabled Abraham to defeat the invading kings.

His primary concern was rescuing Lot, but in the process others were helped. Abraham responded very positively to the king-priest of Salem and gave him a tenth of the spoils. Although his understanding of God may have been different, Melchizedek recognised that God had given victory (God Most High was also the title given to the chief god of the Canaanite pantheon and, although the book of Hebrews gives symbolic significance to Melchizedek, here he is just one of the kings). Abraham's response to Sodom's king is much more negative, either because there was no recognition of God or because Abraham is reacting against general wickedness. However, paradoxically this means that he was given a much larger share of the spoils: Abraham kept nothing that could possibly be seen as belonging to Sodom.

Consider what issues this chapter raises in relation to our dealings with, and gifts to, those from other traditions, religions and moralities.

[1] Acts 20:35

THE VERY GREAT REWARD

'Whatever you do, work at it with all your heart ... since you know that you will receive an inheritance from the Lord as a reward.'[1]

GENESIS 15

The previous chapter could be said to be all about shields and rewards, and this one begins with Abraham learning that the only shield and the only reward he needed was God himself. Lot had needed Abraham to defend him and the kings of Salem and Sodom got their reward from Abraham, but Abraham was to recognise God as his defender. Though at the end of verse 1 the thought may be that his reward comes from God,[2] it is on balance more likely that the meaning is that his reward is God himself.[3] Abraham had not yet grasped that concept. He could not envisage any worthwhile reward that was not dependent on his having a son. It took a long time to dawn on Abraham that the greatest blessing that any person can have is being in relationship with God, and even longer to dawn on Israel in spite of the later covenant formula that expressed the heart of the promise as, 'You will be my people and I will be your God.'

What is most encouraging to me about this chapter is the way that God goes back and leads Abraham on from where he is now – something we all need at times! He starts from Abraham's question and promises both son and land. When Abraham still struggles to work out how this could happen he confirms the promise with a strong and culturally relevant vow-confirming ceremony (the modern equivalent would probably be the actual signing of a contract). In order to help Abraham understand, in order to strengthen their relationship, God allows himself to be involved in this very human ritual. Perhaps we have here a foretaste of the incarnation, of the level of involvement with humanity that God was willing to undertake in order to bring people to himself. Note that the promise of descendants and land did not preclude some very dreadful happenings to those descendants in that land.

What reward am I looking for? Could I pray the prayer, 'Lord, you are my shield, you are my reward, and that is enough'?

[1] Col 3:23,24 [2] 'Your reward will be great', NLT [3] 'I am ... your very great reward', TNIV

RUNNING AWAY

'God gives the desolate a home to live in; he leads out the prisoners to prosperity.'[1]

GENESIS 16

One can understand Sarah's frustration ten years after God promised that Abraham's descendants would inherit the land. Instead of fertility, the Lord had 'kept [her] from having children' (v 2). Was this an occasion when God wanted her to wait and trust, or was he waiting for her to use her own resources and take action? That is always a difficult call for any of us, and Scripture provides instances where each of these alternatives has been God's way forward. However, in this instance Sarah chose the wrong option. She decided that she would only have a child through a surrogate mother so she made the arrangements. As sometimes happens with similar arrangements today, the surrogate mother did not behave as required and Sarah reacted harshly. Her frustration with God, with Hagar and with Abraham makes her come across in this chapter as not very likable. Many of us have been there.

Hagar seems to be a victim here. There is no indication that she had any choice about being used by Sarah and Abraham. Also when, perhaps grasping that laws of the time regarding slaves used for surrogacy would give her a new status, she failed to show the respect that Sarah expected, she was ill-treated. Her running away from a situation where she was treated as an object rather than a person (neither Abraham nor Sarah ever call her by name) is understandable – but she meets God and he does call her by name! She was not the mother of the chosen son, not part of the covenant, but we see clearly here that God cares for outsiders, as we also must. Hagar has the privilege of being the first person in Scripture who is recorded as giving a name to God.

Lord, I know my way of seeing circumstances and people is not yours. Help me to keep seeking your perspective and forgive me when I get it wrong.

---

[1] Ps 68:6, NRSV

IN LINE TO THE THRONE

'We tell you the good news: what God promised our ancestors he has fulfilled for us, their children, by raising up Jesus.'[1]

GENESIS 17

Don't you find it encouraging to see the way in which God keeps reaffirming promises already made? It mattered to God that Abraham and Sarah realised that, in spite of all their mistakes, he still wanted to be in relationship with them, and to use them to work out his purposes. The covenant involves both Abraham and Sarah. Both get a new name, both will be blessed, both are to be part of the royal line. Just in case anyone might think that women are excluded from the covenant because the covenant sign is circumcision, the writer places the message about the blessing for Sarah in the middle of the account about circumcision.

Thirteen years have passed since Ishmael was born, and Abraham has lost any hope that he will have more sons. In fact, he goes out of his way to assure God that he will be quite happy to accept Ishmael as the promised son (although the way the request is phrased shows that he realises this is not God's original plan). But God's response is clear: Ishmael does have his place in the world, and he can even be circumcised and live within the covenant household, but the covenant promise is not to be fulfilled through him. The child of promise is to be born to Sarah. The mother of God's special people was chosen just as much as the father (vs 15,16). The promise of a son to Abraham could perhaps have been fulfilled through Ishmael, but the promise was clearly for Sarah as well (vs 19,21),and Ishmael was not her son. We often see our relationship with God simply in individual terms, but the Bible constantly stresses the need for community. Promises from the Lord can be trusted, even if fulfilment seems long in coming, but we must consider how they affect others, too.

We see here the exclusivism and inclusivism of God's covenant. Are there any situations where we might want to include what should be excluded or exclude what should be included?

[1] Acts 13:32,33

A GOOD LAUGH?

'Tend the flock of God ... willingly ... And when the chief shepherd appears, you will win the crown of glory that never fades away.'[1]

GENESIS 18:1-15

Sometimes it seems Western Christians see hospitality as a secondary gift – something that people can do even if they can't teach, lead or do anything of greater significance. But in both the Old and New Testaments hospitality is seen as a vital indicator of spiritual life. Abraham's visitors were special, but his offer of food, washing and resting facilities came before he knew who they were. Christians in some parts of the world immediately invite visitors to their homes, share with them whatever food is available and generally make sure their needs are met. In other parts of the world, including Britain, the hospitality given by our churches to strangers is often limited to providing a cup of coffee after the service. The teaching and the worship might be great, but the welcome...

In the context of the times, it would have been normal for male guests to eat apart from the family but very abnormal for them to speak about the host's wife and especially to bring her into the conversation; however, as so often in Scripture, God indicates that human cultural customs do not always reflect his perspective. It really mattered that Sarah understood what was going on, that her faith was also tested and stretched. Like Abraham[2] she laughed at the news. God's response to her laugh is often seen as harsh, but we don't know whether the Lord's tone in verse 15 was rebuking or just a gentle, 'Yes you did, and truth matters, but I understand why you laughed so don't worry about it.' However, the question, 'Is anything too hard for the LORD?', which is deliberately left unanswered here, stood as an ongoing challenge to both Sarah and Abraham and remains on the table for each of us to answer in the context of our own lives.

This week, how might I show hospitality to strangers? Am I tempted to think that situations that I might be facing are 'too hard for the Lord'?

[1] 1 Pet 5:2–4, NRSV [2] Gen 17:17

A CHAT BETWEEN FRIENDS

'Truly great friends are hard to find, difficult to leave, and impossible to forget.'[1] Thank God for your faithful friends.

GENESIS 18:16–33

Relationship with God is real! Close friends share thoughts and feelings, allowing one another to know about their concerns. They have confidence in one another and share confidences with one another. Here we see God relating to Abraham in just this way. But shared knowledge is not always easy. Friends of those who have to make difficult decisions – who is to be made redundant, for example – know that only too well.

This section is often presented as Abraham trying to persuade God to be lenient towards Sodom, yet the conversation is not presented that way. Abraham understands the need to punish the wicked but, probably thinking of Lot, he wants to know how far an innocent minority will affect punishment of a guilty majority. (Modern army generals sometimes have the same problem in deciding how many innocent lives should be risked in order for a hugely dangerous group to be destroyed.) Abraham knows God is just and righteous, so would he destroy a city if there are 50 who don't deserve that destruction? God patiently responds to his questioning, agreeing with Abraham that the wicked and righteous do deserve different treatment and letting Abraham know that even ten righteous lives will not be risked in order to remove a wicked regime. Why Abraham stops at ten we don't know, but chapter 19 shows God seeking to save from destruction all who could in any sense be described as righteous.

This chapter makes it clear that even God's close friends don't always understand the way he works. There is nothing at all wrong with questioning God and trying to work out exactly what his intentions are or what his actions mean. In fact, questioning God is sometimes a sign of a really good relationship, and not necessarily a sign of unfaithful doubting.

Do we have questions in our minds that we should be thrashing out with God? It is worth discussing the issues with others of God's friends.

[1] G Randolf

LOT'S CHOICES

'The LORD is gracious and compassionate, slow to anger and rich in love. The LORD is good to all; he has compassion on all he has made.'[1]

GENESIS 19

The question of whether the accusations against Sodom would be proved serious enough to warrant destruction is answered by events. It is interesting that their lack of hospitality receives as much focus as their immorality. Lot had chosen not just to move to Sodom but to associate himself with the city ('my friends', v 7, is literally 'my brothers'). However, they still consider him an alien (v 9). It seems Lot was a weak and greedy man. He had not been completely absorbed into the Sodomite culture, but still retained some values that might be described as righteous – in particular, still recognising the importance of hospitality. Indeed he makes the choice of seeking to protect his guests at the expense of his daughters – a decision which seems horrific to many modern readers; the angels certainly didn't affirm that decision or allow Lot's daughters to be abused in order to save them.

The choice to leave the city was not made easily and was somewhat forced by the angels (v 16). Lot's wife looked back. Whether this indicated that she really didn't want to leave or that she wanted to watch the judgement isn't clear, but whatever her reason the lost time meant that she became a pillar of salt (v 26) – maybe engulfed by the lava. In this kind of situation observation from the sidelines is not possible – the only options are flight or destruction. Lot had spoken of his daughters as if they were not really people, only objects to be used to suit his purposes. It is sad, but perhaps not surprising, that they treat him in the same way. There are lots of unanswered questions in this rather pathetic story, but two things are clear. One is that choices have consequences, the other that God does his best to be merciful and that even pitiful attempts at righteousness are recognised by him.[2]

Lord, if I have an association with evil from which I ought to flee, help me do so without looking back. Make my choices count for good.

[1] Ps 145:8,9 [2] Cf 2 Pet 2:7

GUILT AND INNOCENCE

'Keep your servant also from wilful sins; may they not rule over me. Then I will be blameless, innocent of great transgression.'[1]

GENESIS 20

There is no indication that Abimelek ever had, or even sought, any kind of personal relationship with Abraham's God but there is every indication that he was a good-hearted upright person. Here and in chapter 26 he comes across as having more moral perception than Abraham and Isaac. There is never a hint in the Bible that, humanly speaking, all those who are part of God's people are 'goodies' and all those who are not are 'baddies'. But we need to remember that it is not through our goodness or personal morality that we are saved. Genesis prepares us for the New Testament teaching that salvation is found not in our goodness or in belonging to a particular ethnic, social or even religious group, but only through the grace of God made available through the death and resurrection of Jesus.

The debate about guilt and innocence that we saw in chapter 18 continues here in a different form. Abimelek had sinned unwittingly but he had sinned – or he would have done if God in his grace had not prevented him! Abraham had sinned wittingly, especially in the light of chapter 12's fiasco, but he was still a 'prophet' and could be used to play a part in God's full restoration of Abimelek and his family. (Some scholars think that the incidents of pretending that a wife was a sister in chapters 12, 18 and 27 reflect the same event or combine two stories. However, the details are very different and we all know that making the same mistake twice is not a rare human fault.) The encouragement here is that God knows the hearts and motivations of all, and even when mistakes are made, whether inadvertently or deliberately, he can still bring us back to the right path and continue to use us.

Think about all the 'good' unbelievers you know and about how, despite all your mistakes, God might use you to bring about their full restoration.

---

[1] Ps 19:13

FAMILY FORTUNES

Pray for an eagerness to hear what God wants to say to you personally.

Today's reading starts by highlighting what the Lord does for Sarah and concludes with Abraham worshipping the Lord, the eternal God. The story reminds us that worship arises most naturally when we recognise what God has already done for us.

While Isaac's 'miraculous' birth to the elderly Sarah is an occasion for 'laughter' (note the wordplay on the name Isaac, 'he laughs'), Sarah is troubled by Ishmael's continued presence in the household. The history of this antipathy, which was in part of Sarah's own making, goes back many years. Abraham's initial dismissal of his wife's request that Hagar and Ishmael be expelled is understandable. Previously, God had instructed Hagar to return to Abraham's household and for 14 years Abraham had viewed Ishmael as his son and heir.[1] Amid conflicting choices, Abraham hears and obeys the voice of God. The fulfilment of God's plans can only be achieved through a separation that is painful for those involved. Although the expulsion of Ishmael seems harsh and unfair, it is done with the divine assurance that he will become a great nation. Consequently, when Hagar and Ishmael are without water in the wilderness of Beersheba, God comes to their aid. In spite of having sent them away, he does not abandon them. When conflicting, painful choices demand our obedience, it's important to hear God's voice and trust in his unfailing love.

If Abraham harboured doubts about the wisdom of sending Ishmael away, Abimelek's visit may have offered some reassurance. 'God is with you in all that you do,' the king remarks as he negotiates a friendship treaty with Abraham. Abimelek realises that his own future well-being rests upon having a harmonious relationship with Abraham. We too must view Abraham and his royal descendant, Jesus Christ, positively in order to know God's blessing.[2]

Abraham had to make a difficult choice in sending Ishmael away. Ask God to guide you in the choices you face at present.

[1] *See* Gen 17:18 [2] Gal 3:8–14

CONFLICTING LOYALTIES

Can you recall a time when you were tested by God? How did it challenge your faith and obedience? Talk to God about it.

GENESIS 22

It's very easy to get distracted by the shocking nature of the test that God set Abraham. We don't expect a loving God to require a father to kill his son. Yet, what other test would have been so challenging? Isaac meant everything to Abraham. However, in spite of the horrendous nature of God's request, Abraham believes that everything will somehow work out right. Observe how he tells his servant to anticipate his return with Isaac ('we', v 5).

The test itself is designed to discover how much Abraham reveres and trusts God. His willingness to obey prompts the clear affirmation, 'Now I know that you fear God.' But why did God need to know this? Why does the testing of Abraham's faith bring the story of his life to an important climax? What lies behind this exceptional event? Undoubtedly, the test is intimately linked to the unique divine oath that comes in verses 16–18. This oath, in which God swears by himself, solemnly guarantees the fulfilment of the conditional promises that he had previously given to Abraham.[1] The contents of the divine oath are exceptionally important. First, Abraham's descendants will play a central role in the fulfilment of God's plans for creation. Second, from Abraham will come a royal descendant through whom all the nations of the earth will be blessed.[2] As Paul observes, this latter promise is fulfilled in Jesus Christ.[3] Remarkably, God links the fulfilment of these promises to Abraham's faithful obedience.[4]

By his wholehearted response, Abraham demonstrates the reality of his ongoing faith in God, the very faith by which he had previously been justified.[5] Drawing on this very passage, the apostle James reminds us that faith without works is dead.[6] Our willingness to obey God is a good measure of how much we actually trust him.

Abraham was willing to sacrifice his only son for God. What would you be willing to sacrifice?

[1] Gen 12:1–3 [2] Contrary to TNIV, the original v 17c refers to a singular descendant [3] Gal 3:16 [4] Gen 26:4,5 [5] Gen 15:6 [6] James 2:21–24

LIFE AND DEATH CHOICES

Think back on your life journey with God. How has your knowledge of him influenced the important decisions that you have taken?

GENESIS 23

The death of his wife, Sarah, presented a dilemma. Abraham had to find somewhere to bury her remains. As a foreign migrant, living a semi-nomadic lifestyle, he possessed no land in Canaan, in spite of having arrived near Hebron some six decades earlier. Although Abraham undoubtedly had the financial resources to become a city-dweller, his tent-living lifestyle was determined by his faith in God and not simply the circumstances of life. Had he wished, he could easily have chosen, like his nephew Lot, to settle in one of the local cities. Abraham's hope, however, was to reside in the city of God.[1]

He rejected the generous goodwill gesture of the Hittite inhabitants of Hebron, who saw him as a 'mighty prince' (v 6). He chose, rather, to pay 400 shekels, the price of a dozen able-bodied male slaves, in order to have a permanent right to the burial site. His investment signalled his trust in God. While the Hittites were 'the people of the land' (v 7), Abraham's purchase of Machpelah underlined his deep faith in God's redemptive promises. He believed that one day his descendants would occupy this land as their own. His actions anticipated something that would only happen four centuries later.[2] By buying rather than borrowing a tomb, Abraham established a title deed to part of the land, in anticipation of all that God was yet to do. Abraham's lifestyle and actions offer us an opportunity to reflect on how our faith in God impacts our lives. Do I simply live for the present, or are my actions determined by how I view the future with God?

Do I lay up treasure on earth, or in heaven?[3] Is my citizenship in 'Babylon', or in the 'new Jerusalem'?[4] Like Abraham, we too have important choices to make.

Take a few minutes to reflect on how the reality of your future 'beyond-death' life should influence your 'here-and-now' life.

[1] Heb 11:9,10 [2] Cf Gen 15:13–16 [3] Matt 6:19–21 [4] Ps 87:5,6

A MAN WITH A MISSION

With thanksgiving, reflect on how God has guided you on your spiritual journey.

GENESIS 24:1–33

Abraham's unnamed servant was a man with an unusual mission, for it involved finding a wife for his master's son, a task that would involve a trek of over 500 miles on camelback, from Canaan to northern Mesopotamia. Abraham had entrusted him with this responsibility because he shared his master's commitment to the Lord, and he sincerely believed that God would guide him to a suitable wife for Isaac.

Few stories in the Bible match this account in illustrating the providential activity of God in response to prayer. When the servant arrives at the city of Nahor, he prays that God will so order events that the woman who responds to his request for a drink will be the one for Isaac. While some might dismiss what happens as a remarkable coincidence, the servant readily acknowledges that God has guided him. He bows his head and worships the Lord (v 26). When I need guidance, how open am I to being led by God? Do I believe that God will act in response to my prayer?

While the servant's faith in God is plainly evident, it is supplemented by common sense. His chosen sign is intended to reveal the woman's inner beauty, for he seeks a wife for Isaac who is not only outwardly attractive but also compassionate and generous at heart. To hope that a young woman would give a drink of water to a foreign traveller is not particularly remarkable. To imagine, however, that she would voluntarily water his livestock verges on expecting a miracle, for ten thirsty camels would hardly be satisfied with one jar of water between them. The servant's sign is a successful combination of faith and common sense. It's a helpful reminder that both elements may be necessary when we seek to discover God's will for our lives.

Today's reading gives an interesting insight into the providential activity of God. What lessons might you take from it?

MARRIAGE MADE IN HEAVEN

'Your word is a lamp to my feet and a light for my path.'[1] Praise God for how he directs our lives.

GENESIS 24:34–67

It's amazing how some of my friends first met their life partners. Accounts of how couples come together are frequently surprising. None, however, matches this story of Isaac and Rebekah. No doubt they enjoyed recounting to their grandchildren how God brought them together. Theirs was definitely a marriage made in heaven!

It is interesting to ask what it was that persuaded Rebekah to leave her family. It was not Isaac. He is hardly mentioned in the servant's speech. There is no description of his appearance, achievements or attributes. Rather, Rebekah's life-changing decision, and that of her guardians, Bethuel and Laban, is prompted by the servant's testimony. It is God's actions that shape the response of Nahor's family to Abraham's servant. For this reason the narrator records in detail the servant's account of how he found Rebekah. The God-centred focus of his speech is clearly recognised by Laban and Bethuel, when they respond: 'This is from the LORD' (v 50). Remarkably, Rebekah commits herself to her future partner on the basis of who God is, not what Isaac is like. Strange as it may seem, this is a marriage that originated out of a deep love for God rather than for a human partner. Rebekah, however, does not regret her decision. If you had been Rebekah, how would you have responded? Will you commit yourself now to an uncertain future, confident in God's goodness and his clear leading?

In trusting God, Rebekah resembles Abraham. Like Abraham, she hears the call of God to leave her family and homeland. Like Abraham, she goes in faith, believing that she will play a special role in the fulfilment of God's purposes. She is undoubtedly the perfect match for Isaac, a point emphasised by the way in which her family's blessing (v 60) echoes God's oath to Abraham in 22:16–18.

Rebekah's faith was no less than that of Abraham. Think over what you can learn from both of them about having a relationship with God.

[1] Ps 119:105

CONTROL FREAKS

'Take your everyday, ordinary life – your sleeping, eating, going-to-work, and walking-around life – and place it before God as an offering.'[1]

GENESIS 25:1–11,19–34

Recently I saw a newspaper article which described the need for young parents to undergo training in how to give love and affection to their children! How corrupt is a society when it has lost the instinct for such things? Abraham apparently needed no such training – he understood God's model of fatherhood. We know how much he cherished Isaac, but he retained a fatherly concern for Ishmael.[2] We know he loved Sarah, but Keturah's children were his too and he made provision for them. Parents (physical and spiritual) must love their children in practical ways if they also want to assert their authority over them. A parent's love is an important source of parental honour. Don't just quote the commandment[3] – consider: have I ever given my offspring reason to doubt my love for them? Ishmael may have felt rejected, but the parent–child cycle of love and honour was so firmly established that he returned to mourn with Isaac when Abraham died (v 9).

Our second passage is a timely reminder for us that God is sovereign over every aspect of life. We live in an age of control and immediacy. We expect to be able to have or do anything we like, subject only to having sufficient cash. The clumsy manipulation of fertility that is IVF fools us into thinking we have control. The reluctance to wait for anything we desire leads to the burden of unnecessary debt. In contrast, we see Isaac and Rebekah turning to God to find answers to their questions and have their deepest needs met. These parents knew that God had brought them together and planned to bless them. But look at the timescale: 20 years between marriage and the birth of their first child! Did Isaac offer up his prayer regularly for 19 years?

Re-examine your life. Who or what is in control? Pray Psalm 139:23,24 so that God might show you.

---

[1] Rom 12:1, *The Message* [2] Gen 21:11 [3] Exod 20:12

DEVIL IN THE DETAIL

Thank Christ for his promise: 'I'll be with you as you do this, day after day after day, right up to the end of the age.'[1]

GENESIS 26:1–33

In this chapter we learn a lot about Isaac's developing character and relationship with God. He inherits more than his father's possessions;[2] more significantly, God appears to Isaac and confirms his inheritance of the divine promises made to his father Abraham. Isaac was obedient to God in choosing a place for his family to survive the famine, but he didn't trust God to protect him from men who might covet his wife. God had been so direct: 'I will be with you and will bless you' (v 3), but Isaac allowed fear and selfishness to compromise his integrity. He was afraid to name Rebekah as his wife and was prepared to risk her virtue for his personal safety. Perhaps he thought his deception was just a detail – not as important as the 'big' issues?

Are you a leader (of a household or a fellowship) who finds it relatively straightforward to trust God with the big things in life, but struggles to hand over the minutiae? You follow God's leading when it comes to a job, a place to live and where to worship, but take matters into your own hands when it comes to preparing your tax return (on your income, you need every penny), obeying the speed limit (can't be late for church again) and submitting to copyright law (sure, I'm copying this DVD, but the youth group can't afford to buy every resource it needs).

Ironically, it is the Philistine king Abimelek who points out Isaac's foolishness: 'You would have been responsible for bringing guilt down on us' (v 10, *The Message*). Don't ever think that God's people have a monopoly on virtue! We must live with integrity in every matter, no matter how small it seems – the consequences of 'small' sins are always more far-reaching than we realise.

Living God's way in every detail requires great discernment, developing with experience over time. Reflect on Psalm 19:12,13 and pray that hidden faults don't lead to 'great transgression'.

[1] Matt 28:20, *The Message* [2] Gen 25:5

KNOWING OR TRUSTING

Are you seeking God's will? Of one thing you may be sure: 'It is God's will that you should be sanctified.'[1] Pray that he will direct your thoughts today.

GENESIS 26:34 – 27:29

The more I reflect on this passage, the less certain I am about what it might be teaching me about God's will and how to live as his servant today. Jacob lies, deceives and dishonours his father. Hundreds of years later, God gave the people of Israel laws that expressly prohibited this kind of behaviour, so it is reasonable for us to believe that it is not the behaviour God desires. Perhaps Rebekah should take responsibility. She directed Jacob in the deceit, despite his reservations, and invited the risk of curse upon herself should things go badly. She had been expressly told by God that 'the elder will serve the younger',[2] and so perhaps she believed that she was doing what God wanted in subverting her husband's intent.

Was the word Rebekah received an indicator of God's perfect will or simply God's foreknowledge of what was going to happen? Traditionally, Jews and Christians hold that Jacob was God's chosen vessel through whom the nation of Israel would be established and the blessing of all nations would be transmitted. It is difficult for us to know exactly how God was working out his purposes in all this. It is even more difficult for us to discern a godly example for our own lives! Perhaps the most important things to remember are that God knows the end from the beginning,[3] that his ways are beyond tracing out, and that he is working for the good of those who love him. We can take heart in these certainties and pray to be transformed by the renewing of our minds so that we will know God's good, pleasing and perfect will. Then we have the best hope of serving him in accordance with his character.

Thank God for the absolute certainties of his love, faithfulness and goodness, and practise childlike faith as you reflect on the mysteries too.

---

1 1 Thess 4:3a **2** Gen 25:23 **3** Isa 46:10; Rom 11:33; 8:28; 12:2

CONSEQUENCES

Pray that the eyes of your heart may be enlightened, so that you will know God's incomparably great power in all who believe.

In 1935, the Cane Toad was introduced into Australia to control the native Cane Beetle, a threat to sugar cane production. It wasn't long before the toad's destructive impact on the native ecology became apparent. Despite best intentions, sometimes our actions produce unforeseen and unfortunate consequences.

After recovering from the initial grief and despair at losing his father's blessing, Esau becomes vengeful and homicidal, risking a blood feud that had the potential to destroy the family line (v 45). Rebekah doesn't seem to have anticipated that as a consequence of her actions. Trying to get things under control, she proposes to Isaac that Jacob is sent away to find a wife among her brother's family. She believes she can contain the situation; but she can't. Verse 45 implies that she thought Esau would get over it relatively quickly: when he had settled down she would call Jacob back and they would all be one happy family. But it was not to be: it would be 20 years before Jacob returned to his father's family. Rebekah died without ever seeing her favourite son again. Doubtless she didn't anticipate that either. Jacob laboured 20 years for a deceitful uncle and lived in fear of Esau's wrath right up until the next time they met.

We need to commit our lives to careful, reflective decision making, recognising the limit of our control over situations as well as the omnipotence of our sovereign God. A consumer-centred culture places me and you at the centre of every decision we encounter. The old adage, 'What's in it for me?' drives every marketing campaign. With God out of the picture, we only make a mess of things, however noble our intentions. Only with Spirit-filled hearts and eyes fixed on Christ can we begin to act rightly.

One aspect of growing in faith is committing your way to the Lord and trusting him. Do that now.

EPIPHANY AND THEOPHANY

'He found him at Bethel and talked with him there.'[1] Call to mind a time when God revealed himself to you in a dramatic way, and worship him afresh.

GENESIS 28:10–22

As far as we know, this is Jacob's first recorded, direct encounter with the God of Abraham and Isaac. His reaction is marked by fear, awe and a powerful sense of the presence of God: 'How awesome is this place!' (v 17). Jacob would have heard his grandfather and father speak of God's covenant with them, but stories remain stories until we have some sort of personal encounter with the living God. For Jacob, this encounter changed his life.

Perhaps, like me, you were blessed with godly parents and a Christian upbringing. I reached adulthood with sound doctrine but limited passion for my Saviour King. But in my early twenties, I had a profound encounter with God (not a dream, mind, and no theophany for me). Over several months I became painfully aware of how desperately sinful I was and how much I needed God's grace and mercy. This changed my life.

In a similar way, this dream was a turning point for Jacob. He still uses the conditional 'if' as he prays to God, but in a sense he is only laying hold of the promises God made first to him. In so doing, Jacob reveals his deepest concerns as he leaves the familiar and journeys into the unknown: that God will be with him, watch over him and give him food and clothing – a poignant expression of his dependence on God for everything.

A sense of place has been very important to the patriarchs and the Hebrew people ever since. They were promised land and longed to build God's house there. Under the new covenant, every believer is the temple of the Holy Spirit[2] and Jesus promised that when we meet together, we can say that God 'is in this place'.[3] How awesome!

Pray specifically for the fellowship you are a part of: that when people visit they may know that God is among you.

---

[1] Hos 12:4b [2] 1 Cor 6:19 [3] *See* Matt 18:20; 1 Cor 14:25

TRAVELLING MERCIES

Pray or sing: 'Through many dangers, toils and snares, I have already come; 'tis grace hath brought me safe thus far, and grace will lead me home.'[1]

GENESIS 29:1–14a

This well-known narrative doesn't mention God, but is still a powerful example of his mercy and faithfulness. Haran is about 440 miles from Beersheba as the crow flies, so we can assume Jacob's journey took at least three weeks. Jacob left the only home he had ever known, threatened with death by his twin brother, sleeping rough and probably travelling alone. His prayer at Bethel[2] reveals both his fear and anxiety on the one hand, and his decision to acknowledge God on the other. Then he arrives at a well near his destination. In the arid Near East, wells were enormously significant, both for survival and as places of meeting, community and family. Imagine the significance of this account to the first hearers. They had just heard God's promise of protection to Jacob in Bethel: 'I am with you and will watch over you wherever you go'.[3] Almost immediately, fulfilment of the promise begins. A safe arrival at a well – literally and symbolically a place of provision: water, flocks, food, family and ultimately a wife!

Notice how Jacob's character is developing after removal from a controlling mother, a personal encounter with God and weeks on the road. It is reasonable to assume he was tired and hungry, but his first act on reaching Haran is to help the locals with their work. The stone covering the well was considered too large for the shepherds already present and they had to wait till more arrived before watering the sheep. Nevertheless, Jacob sets himself to work before any formalities are complete, performing the impressive feat of uncovering the well and even then not resting until he has watered his uncle's sheep. Jacob takes nothing for granted and works hard for the warm welcome he receives from Laban.

God's protection is for all who dwell in his shelter. Review Psalm 91:14–16 and prayerfully consider your role: to love God, acknowledge his name and call upon him.

---

[1] From 'Amazing Grace', John Newton, 1725–1807 [2] Gen 28:20–22
[3] Gen 28:15

LOVE CHANGES EVERYTHING

'O Lord, You're beautiful, Your face is all I seek ... please light the fire that önce burned bright and clear; replace the lamp of my first love.'[1]

GENESIS 29:14b–30

'Jacob was in love with Rachel ...' (v 18) and to him the universe adjusted and time stood still: everything changed. Seven years seemed like only a few days because he loved and valued her so highly that any price seemed small. Call to mind your first time of loving God deeply, completely and with abandon. Perhaps it was as a young person. Perhaps it was last week. Either way, the Scriptures recognise the extraordinary power of first love and challenge us not to forget it.[2] In Revelation, Jesus calls the Ephesian church to repentance, accusing them of forsaking their first love and commanding them to 'do the things you did at first'.[3] God loves it when we love him passionately.

Notice Jacob's submission to Laban in accepting the revised deal. Why and how did he do this? I like to think that he was learning discretion. Jacob had been promised protection and provision by God more than seven years earlier. When we believe God, acknowledge him and trust all his promises, it relieves us of having to administer, enforce or manipulate justice ourselves. We know that Jacob had been called according to God's purpose, so perhaps he was learning to trust to that. How difficult it is to submit to a deceitful and manipulative master like Laban. In my study of Jesus' teaching, I have recently been reminded of his words in the Sermon on the Mount, 'Do not resist an evil person'. I have felt somewhat taken advantage of at times this year, and after remembering this teaching have more than once decided to submit to the will of the other party. Surprisingly, I experienced a strong sense of freedom and peace after making this choice, and learned a little more about trusting God.

Reflect on any injustice you may have suffered and how you chose to react. Did you turn the other cheek and submit, or did you take the easy way out?

[1] Keith Green © 1980 Birdwing Music/BMG songs/Ears to Hear Music/EMI Christian Music Publishing [2] Jer 2:2 [3] Rev 2:4,5; Rom 8:28; Matt 5:39

BY HOOK OR BY CROOK

If you have a hymn book, meditate on 'God moves in a mysterious way' by William Cowper (1731–1800). If not, reflect on Isaiah 55:8,9 instead.

GENESIS 29:31 – 30:24

How gracious and merciful God is! Amid all the foolishness, fear and weakness of Jacob, Leah and Rachel, God is working his purposes out, fulfilling his promises to Abraham, Isaac and Jacob, and establishing the building blocks for his holy nation. What a good thing that 'it is on divine mercy, not human effort, that the hope of the world's salvation rests'.[1] The people in this narrative attribute various actions and interests to God, but I don't find them all convincing. Let's look today at what the narrator has to say about God in this passage. Whether the author was Moses or another godly person, this scripture was written under the guidance and inspiration of the Holy Spirit.[2]

'The LORD saw' (29:31) and 'God listened' (30:17): such characteristics of God are evident throughout Scripture. Perhaps Moses (if it was he) could recall his first encounter with God: 'I have indeed seen the misery of my people in Egypt. I have heard them crying out ...'[3] God sees our lives and hears our petitions. In biblical terms, 'God remembered' (v 22) is no indication of a propensity for forgetfulness on God's part. Rather it is an expression of his loving concern and care for his people, especially when they call out to him in humility. Finally, more than once, we are told that God 'enabled her to conceive' and are reminded of God's complete sovereignty over the mysteries of life and fertility – a sovereignty that Jacob has learned to acknowledge and which his wives sometimes attribute rightly. IVF might be more scientific than mandrakes, but most doctors will admit that ultimately there are no guarantees. Do such thoughts concern you (that your control over circumstances is so limited) or comfort you (that God's sovereignty is not)?

Do you know a couple who are trying to start a family? Pray for them today – that they will be blessed and grow in trust in God.

---

[1] GJ Wenham, *New Bible Commentary 21st Century Edition*, IVP, 1994, p81
[2] 2 Tim 3:16,17; 2 Pet 1:20,21 [3] Exod 3:7; *see eg* Neh 13:31b

PERFECT TIMING

'You see, at just the right time, when we were still powerless, Christ died for the ungodly.'[1] Use this verse as a stimulus to offer up thanks and praise.

GENESIS 30:25 – 31:21

Learning to discern God's will for my life is a big enough challenge, but to know when to do it is something I am still learning. I once had a job which wasn't ideal for me and which I wanted to leave. I prayed almost daily for the opportunity to leave, but no job applications proved fruitful. I was so frustrated. Over a number of years, my prayer to depart gradually changed into a prayer to discern and submit to God's timetable, learning to acknowledge him in all my ways.[2] In retrospect, I can see that I had some important lessons to learn, but when the day to depart arrived God's timing was clear.

Jacob had been clearly told at Bethel that it was God's intention for him to return to his father's land.[3] He now felt ready to return – but this was his timing, not God's. Perhaps there were lessons he still needed to learn. Perhaps he simply needed six more years in Haran to prosper. The narrator doesn't explain it to us and God doesn't appear to have explained it to Jacob either. Was he frustrated?

The story (possibly apocryphal) is told of a Thai brothel manager who became a Christian. As he embarked on his new life, the first issue he felt convicted to address was his habit of watering down the drinks in the bar! God has a unique way of changing each one of us (if we let him), little by little. Jacob still attempted to make decisions without reference to God, still resorted to superstition or magic to manipulate circumstances and still deceived his uncle when he finally departed. However, he had learned at least one crucial lesson. He had learned to acknowledge God as the source of his blessing and prosperity (31:5,9).

God's people ought to be a blessing to others, wherever he places them. However imperfect your circumstances, consider how you might be a blessing to others today.

---

[1] Rom 5:6 [2] Prov 3:5,6 [3] Gen 28:15; see Gen 30:27

BLESSINGS IN THE DETAIL

Pray the words of Micah 7:18–20 as you prepare to meet God, remembering God's promise to pardon sin and be true to all his inheritance.

GENESIS 31:22–42

How much has Jacob really changed over 20 years? We have read how he had a personal encounter with God at Bethel, how he had learned to acknowledge God (at times) and had learned to follow God's general call but, as we read yesterday, he didn't always know when to act, and in today's reading it is clear that he still hasn't learned how to act either. It seems that in the smaller matters, the areas which God left to Jacob's discretion, Jacob still put more faith in his wits and deceitful manipulation of circumstances than in God's providential intervention. What a contrast to his grandfather Abraham, who believed, trusted and obeyed God even when required to do things that seemed to make no sense at all. When challenged to sacrifice Isaac as a burnt offering,[1] Abraham obeyed, reasoning that God could raise the dead[2] and so keep the promise that it was through Isaac that his offspring would be reckoned.[3] How would Jacob have approached such a test? Would he have looked for a loophole? What trick might he have resorted to in order to do as God requested without really trusting God?

Jacob obeyed God by leaving Laban 'at once' (v 13), but did so secretly and deceitfully. He could have presented his case to Laban (vs 38–42) before his departure, demonstrating a more godly way of relating to difficult people and retaining greater honour in the eyes of his relatives, wives and even himself. Even if his fears had been realised (v 31), God could have intervened to protect Jacob and his family in Haran rather than needing to intervene in Gilead. The way Jacob chose to leave still required God's intervention, but left Jacob without the blessing that comes from trusting God in the face of difficult situations.

Reflect on what God is calling you to do, and ask him for the wisdom and courage to do it his way, not yours.

[1] Gen 22 [2] Heb 11:19 [3] Gen 21:12

TRUSTING THE UNWORTHY

'It is better to be sometimes cheated than never to have trusted.'[1]
How serious is the erosion of trust in the world today? How can it
be recovered?

GENESIS 31:43–45

Over the course of the 20 years during which Jacob worked for
Laban, their relationship steadily deteriorated. Part of the problem
was that they were so much alike: both were consummate cheats
and liars, and they had repeatedly deceived each other. At this
point, after Jacob had cunningly absconded with Laban's daughters,
grandchildren, flocks and household gods, their relationship was
at an all-time low. They trade anger and accusations at length (*see*
vs 26–42), but the question now is, how could either of them ever
trust each other again?

So when these two unreliable rogues at last strike an agreement of
fair dealing and mutual protection, they devise their own elaborate
and uneasy covenant-making ceremony: involving the erection of
not one but two stone pillars, calling upon multiple witnesses (v 53),
offering sacrifices and making solemn oaths before God – and other
gods just in case. God is addressed as 'the Fear' (v 53; *cf* v 42), a name
which carries a sense of threat and foreboding – ultimately he's the
only source of trust left.

As I was thinking about this passage in view of the current
widespread crisis of trust in the world – in government, banking and
business, the media, the church – I came upon this prayer, written
by Temple Gairdner[2] on the eve of his wedding. It provides us with
a helpful way of praying about the development of trust in all our
relationships today.

'That I may come near to her, draw me nearer to thee than to her; that
I may know her, make me to know thee more than her; that I may love
her with the perfect love of a perfectly whole heart, cause me to love
thee more and most of all. Amen. Amen.'[3]

1 Samuel Johnson, 1709–84 2 Missionary and Arabic scholar, 1873–1928
3 Quoted by M Magdalen in *The Hidden Face of Jesus*, DL&T, 1994, pp164,165

PREPARING TO MEET ESAU

'We change when the pain of remaining the same is greater than the pain of changing.'[1] Why do you think Jacob wants to be reconciled with Esau?

GENESIS 32:1–21

Having settled a truce with Laban, Jacob now prepares to patch things up with his estranged brother Esau, from whose murderous intentions he had fled previously (27:41-45). But why? This could well be a case of 'out of the frying pan and into the fire'. As readers, we've become fully acquainted with Jacob's wily ways – what's he really up to? Jacob first sends his servants to Esau with an odd message of excessive deference (vs 4,5). When they return with news of the size of Esau's force, Jacob immediately divides his camp to minimise any losses (vs 7,8).

Then he prays. (Noted Old Testament scholar Claus Westermann regards this prayer as the climax of Genesis 31-33.[2]) Jacob lays bare his soul before God and reveals his genuine feelings of extreme distress.[3] As the Scottish minister Robert Murray M'Cheyne[4] has observed, 'A man is what he is on his knees before God, and nothing more.' The way Jacob addresses God (v 9) implicitly calls to mind all that God had done for his grandfather and father. Then Jacob explicitly sets out the logic of his case: God had made the promise; he had prospered under God's mercy and grace; now Jacob (and everyone with him) was in mortal danger; God would have to keep his promise. 'To keep to his word the God who keeps his word is the way of all true prayer.'[5] Having sought God's help in prayer, Jacob nevertheless hedges his bets by making careful and calculated plans to overwhelm Esau with an abundance of gifts (vs 13-21). Such impressive generosity might not merely serve to appease Esau, but giving the herds would keep his men occupied, impede any travel and position some of Jacob's servants within his brother's camp. Jacob remains an all-too-human mixture of faith, fear and doubt.

'I do believe; help me overcome my unbelief!'[6]

[1] Alcoholics Anonymous [2] *Genesis: A Practical Commentary*, T&I; Eerdmans, 1987, p226 [3] *See* Judg 2:15; 10:9, 1 Sam 30:6 [4] 1813–43 [5] F Delitzsch, *Genesis*, T&T Clark, 1888, vol 2, p202 [6] Mark 9:24

BEWILDERED GYMNAST[1]

'A strange adventure, mysterious from beginning to end, breathtakingly beautiful ... Philosophers, poets, rabbis and storytellers, all have yearned to shed light on the enigmatic event that took place that night.'[1]

GENESIS 32:22–32

Suddenly the story changes. From out of nowhere, Jacob is attacked. He wrestles with his unidentified assailant all night. In the struggle, he is wounded, but he refuses to let go of his attacker until he is blessed. The whole extraordinary incident is summed up in verse 30: 'I saw God face to face, and yet my life was spared.'[3] What's going on here? Biblical storytelling and systematic theology don't always sit comfortably together. Commentators, preachers and poets have a field day with this passage. The context suggests that the story is intended to be at least part of the answer to Jacob's prayer in 32:9–11. The answer comes not through waiting passively for God to remove the threat posed by Esau, but by being locked in close combat with a stranger. Jacob asks for a blessing from his mysterious opponent, as he had once before asked of his aged, blind father, but now things are different.

Then Jacob had received a blessing by trickery, but now he discovers that a blessing can only be obtained – daringly from God – through costly personal struggle. The blessing that Jacob receives is symbolised by the new name given to him. In the ancient world a name was more than a label of identity. The new name signified a complete change in Jacob's character. Jacob the cheat will for ever after be known as Israel, someone who is united with God in intimate and mature fellowship – an inherent blessing and a blessing to others. How willing are you to endure costly personal struggle with God in order to receive his blessing? What wounds has he left you with that make you constantly dependent upon him? Since meeting God, what is your new identity in him?

To ponder: 'On the cross too there is wrestling ... there is wounding to the point of death, the identity of a people and of God is at stake, and there is eventual blessing.'[4]

[1] E Dickinson, 'A little East of Jordan' [2] E Wiesel, *Messengers of God*, Random House, 1976, p176 [3] *See* Exod 33:20 [4] D Ford, *Self and Salvation*, CUP, 1999, p195

FORGIVE AND LIVE

'When thou dost ask me blessing, I'll kneel down / And ask of thee forgiveness: so we'll live, / And pray, and sing, and tell old tales, and laugh / At gilded butterflies.'[1]

GENESIS 33

Jacob's wrestling with God and his reconciliation with Esau are clearly connected, and possibly causal. Jacob was held in God's fearsome embrace before he received his brother's embrace of forgiveness. One exceptional face-to-face encounter has led to another (v 11).

This meeting between the two estranged brothers is at first solemn and tense. Jacob proceeds cautiously and comes within sight of Esau. Mistrust is often broken down slowly, step by step (vs 1–3). The new man, Israel, is humble and contrite,[2] and eager to make full reparations to his brother (v 10). Esau too is a changed man. Mellowed by middle age or simply overcome by a sense of immediate love, he movingly offers Jacob full and free pardon. Here is a warm and joyful picture of grace and forgiveness, and it surely paints the background to Jesus' great parable of the prodigal son.[3] Anyone with direct experience of ongoing, intractable family estrangement might find such a scene hard to imagine, yet at the same time, long for it with all their heart.[4] Take time to use it as an aid to prayer, visualising the scene with your own characters, and step-by-step moving the action along the way of reconciliation, from uneasy encounter to loving embrace.

The story is not unrealistic. Jacob still hesitates and prevaricates (vs 13,14). Mistrust, mixed motives and painful memories linger on, but God has kept his promise of blessing and real progress has been made: Israel has settled in Canaan (vs 18–20), and Jacob and Esau are brothers in arms again.

A prayer for the healing of a relationship: 'Christ between us / to sever and to reconcile, / to shield us from the sin in one another, / to bless all that is good and true, / to cleanse from pride, possessiveness, lust, / to give laughter, tears, understanding and peace.'[5]

---

[1] King Lear, Act V, scene iii [2] see Ps 51:17 [3] Luke 15:11–32; cf Rom 5:1–8
[4] See www.cfhscotland.org.uk/resources [5] Ian Cowie

HEART OF DARKNESS

'To the lost Christ shows his face; / To the unloved he gives his embrace: / To those who cry in pain or disgrace, / Christ makes with his friends a touching place.'[1]

GENESIS 34

In 1994 during the Rwandan civil war, *The Times* carried a photo of a little Tutsi girl. She had been orphaned and she had a terrible head injury following a machete attack. Many similar photos appeared that year but this one stays in my memory because the caption gave the name of the little girl: Agnes. Have you noticed how rarely those 'disaster portraits' from the developing world actually name the subjects? I wonder if it's to guard their dignity or ours, to protect us from feeling too involved in other people's suffering?

Not long after Jacob and his tribe have begun to settle in the new land, they run into trouble. Dinah, his daughter, is raped by Shechem, a Canaanite (v 2). What could be done? Any personal concerns are soon superseded by tribal and religious questions. Dinah is never mentioned again. Shechem and his father suggest a pragmatic compromise – intermarrying with their tribe (vs 8-12). Dinah's brothers Simeon and Levi, however, become fixated with her sexual violation (v 31) and take on her disgrace as if it were their own. So they wreak a terrible and truly disgraceful act of vengeance not just on Shechem but on the whole tribe (vs 25-29).

I feel sadness and despair over this ancient story. Why is Jacob so passive and quiet? What kind of a society can be so violent and destructive in its pursuit of justice and religious purity? Then I come across a headline in the *Church Times*, 'A shameful silence', and a report by Elaine Storkey, president of Tearfund, tells me that women in the Democratic Republic of Congo are being routinely raped, mutilated and tortured in the course of a religious and tribal war, but that some Christian relief work is bringing healing and hope. Lord, have mercy.

'For you were once darkness, but now you are light in the Lord. Live as children of light ... and find out what pleases the Lord.'[2]

---

[1] John Bell and Graham Maule, 'Touching Place', WGrG, Iona Community, 1989
[2] Eph 5:8–10

IN MY END, MY BEGINNING

Blessed be God 'who answered me in ... my distress and who has been with me wherever I have gone'.[1]

As Jacob nears the end of his journey, God calls him to return to Bethel (v 1; *cf* 27:43) as a way of revisiting his entire past. (The references to Jacob's earlier life as recorded in Genesis 25-30 are too numerous to list, but take a look yourself.) At Bethel, where he has experienced the true and living God, Jacob will have the opportunity to lead his people in worship and witness, as well as fulfilling his vow and giving thanks to God for his protection and providential care (v 3). Once again, God makes himself known to Jacob at Bethel, and he provides the strongest expression of his blessing so far, summing up and expanding what had been promised earlier (vs 9-12; *cf* 28:3,4, 13-15). The covenant with Abraham[2] is also reiterated – descendants in abundance and a homeland at last.

This time, God makes himself known to Jacob as 'God Almighty', El Shaddai (v 11) – the name by which God had addressed Abraham, and which Isaac had invoked when he conferred his blessing on Jacob. Now Jacob hears the name from God himself. He can now fill the name with solid content – guidance, protection, provision and faithfulness – and there is the promise of more to come.

'When is the Search ended? In one sense, it is finished when our hand, stretched out to God in the name of his appointed mediator Jesus Christ, feels the answering grasp and knows that he is there. But in another sense the searching never ends, for the first discovery is quickly followed by another, and so it goes on. To find that he is, is the mere starting point of our search. We are lured on to explore what he is, and that search is never finished, and it grows more thrilling the farther one proceeds.'[3]

When you look back on your own journey of faith, what meaning does the name God Almighty have for you?

---

[1] Gen 35:3 [2] Gen 17:1–8; 28:3 [3] Isabel Kuhn, *By Searching*, OMF, 1957, p79

A FRUITFUL FAMILY TREE

Lord, I thank you for my family: the Jacobs, the Esaus, the Rachels and the Reubens.

GENESIS 35:16 – 36:8

'How fruitful are the seeming barren places of Scripture … Wheresoever the surface of God's Word doth not laugh and sing with corn, there the heart thereof within is merry with mines, affording, where not plain matter, hidden mysteries.'[1] Since the advent of the internet, research into family trees has grown in popularity. Biblical genealogies, however, still struggle to find an appreciative audience. The lists of Jacob's and Esau's families gave their descendants – including us – a clear and secure identity within the gracious purposes of God and provide inescapable evidence of God's inclusive vision. 'We are required by this carefully placed text to recognise the large vision of Genesis,' notes Walter Brueggemann in *Genesis*. 'This book of gracious beginnings belongs to Muslims (children of Esau) as well as to Jews and Christians (children of Jacob).'[2]

So Reuben is included, despite his act of incest (v 22). Simeon and Levi, too, despite their destructive vengeance against the Shechemites (v 23; cf 34:25-29). And perhaps the most remarkable inclusion is Esau and his whole tribe, the Edomites (36:1-8). We know that Esau had forfeited the blessings of his birthright (27:30-40), and the narrative has been progressively focusing on Jacob and his descendants. Informed by Malachi 1:2,3 and Romans 9:13, we might harbour a negative view of him, but the writer of Genesis has portrayed Esau in a better and 'more equal light'. Recall his dignity, love and grace when he is reconciled with Jacob (ch 33). Still, the divine promises are made to Jacob and not to Esau. Jacob and his descendants are destined for the Promised Land, while Esau must go in a different direction, to Seir (v 8). The brothers go their separate ways, 'participants not in the promise but in the mercy which the promise shows forth' (Martin Luther).[3]

'There is nothing we can do to make God love us more. There is nothing we can do to make God love us less.'[4]

[1] T Fuller, 'Scriptural Observation XVI', in *Good Thoughts in Bad Times*, 1645
[2] *Genesis, Interpretation*; J Knox Press, 1982, p286 [3] Quoted by Brueggemann
[4] P Yancey, *What's So Amazing About Grace?*, Zondervan, 2002

A DREAMY TEENAGER?

Prepare for today's reading by giving thanks to God for family members who have been especially supportive of you.

GENESIS 37:1–11

This is no happy family. As a teenager, Joseph alienates himself from his brothers by 'grassing' on them to his father. To complicate matters further, Jacob's preferential treatment of Joseph fuels his brothers' antagonism towards him. An already tense situation is not helped when Joseph dreams that his brothers will bow down to him. When Joseph tells of a second dream in which his whole family worships him, even his father Jacob is offended. Yet, in the process of rebuking Joseph, Jacob takes careful note of what his favourite son has said. We are expected to anticipate something special regarding Joseph.

Our automatic reaction is to analyse the dysfunctional nature of this family. We are surely meant to learn from their shortcomings. Paternal favouritism quickly breeds jealousy, and spoiled teenagers can easily become captivated by their own importance and despise everyone else. Are there lessons about human relationships that I might learn from reflecting on this family? Yet something more profound is being communicated here, as we are introduced to Joseph and his brothers. If we have read the preceding chapters, we can see that Joseph's royal aspirations are not simply the delusions of a pretentious teenager. From Abraham onwards, the author of Genesis has been especially interested in tracing a line of descendants from whom will come a special king. The promise of royal descendants begins with Abraham[1] and continues through Isaac to Jacob.[2] At each stage an older brother is passed over in favour of a younger sibling (Ishmael in favour of Isaac; Esau in favour of Jacob). In the light of his family history, Joseph's dreams take on special significance. While later we discover that God uses Joseph to save many people, ultimately the story of Joseph points forward to Jesus, the future King through whom God restores wayward humanity to himself.

Personal ambitions can create conflict within a family. Can you think of a situation that needs your prayers just now?

[1] Gen 17:6 [2] Gen 27:29

DREAM TO NIGHTMARE

Lord of light and truth, shine into my darkness and dispel all deceit and falsehood.

GENESIS 37:12–36

The brothers didn't forget Joseph's dreams. When the opportunity arises, they conspire together to murder 'that dreamer'. Well away from their father's oversight, they saw the unexpected arrival of Joseph as an opportunity to rid themselves of their number one enemy. Yet, while they collectively decided to kill Joseph, the unexpected interventions of two brothers resulted in his life being spared. Note carefully what motivated Reuben and Judah.

Reuben is anxious to regain his father's approval. As Jacob's firstborn son, Reuben should have been heir to the divinely promised royal line. However, his unseemly relationship with Bilhah, his father's servant-wife[1], had jeopardised his status as firstborn son. Joseph became the beneficiary and appears to have been designated as heir by his father. Reuben may have hoped that his rescue of Joseph might lead to his own reinstatement as heir: his rescue of Joseph might help him to regain his lost status. Judah's intervention was also motivated by selfishness. He, however, saw an easy opportunity to enrich himself and his brothers. Masking his real motive with a highly ironic reference to Joseph as 'our brother, our own flesh' (v 27), he persuaded his brothers to sell Joseph to traders en route to Egypt. Judah's eye for a 'quick buck' is a solemn reminder of how easily the desire for wealth can starve us of compassion for others. The callousness of the brothers comes to a climax as they deceive their father. While Jacob had years earlier used a goat's skin to hoodwink his own father, now his sons use goat's blood to trick him. Reflect on the hardness of the brothers' hearts as they watch their father grieve so bitterly for Joseph. What would you have done in their place?

Prayerfully consider this question: Are my desires, motives and actions really any different from those of Joseph's brothers?

---

[1] Gen 35:22

UNMASKED

Take a little time to give thanks to God for how your life has been transformed by his grace and love.

GENESIS 38

The spotlight turns unexpectedly from Joseph to Judah. Judah might well have wished that he had remained in the shadows. This is not what you would call family-friendly reading, but the events of this chapter are integral to understanding the rest of Genesis. Two themes are especially important: the continuation of Judah's family line and the transformation of Judah's character. Binding these together is Tamar, Judah's daughter-in-law.

Initially, Tamar appears to be a tragic source of misfortune for Judah's family. First Er and then Onan die after being married to her. While custom dictated that she should become the wife of Shelah, Judah intervened and uncaringly sent her back to her own family. He wanted nothing more to do with her. Yet, when he later hears that she has become pregnant through immoral behaviour, he swiftly pronounces with self-righteous indignation that she should be burnt to death. However, on discovering that he is responsible for her pregnancy, Judah's hypocrisy is unmasked. He suddenly sees himself as he truly is. Tamar's righteousness exceeds his own (v 26). This moment of self-discovery transforms Judah and he becomes a new man, a fact demonstrated later by his willingness to take the place of Benjamin and become a slave in Egypt.[1]

The description of the twin boys being born is bizarre. Zerah, whom the midwife marks with a scarlet thread as the firstborn, is pushed aside by Perez. In a book that sets special store by younger brothers attaining the privileges of the firstborn, this event is highly significant. The divinely promised royal line will be traced through Perez, a fact confirmed in the book of Ruth.[2] With good reason, Tamar is recalled by Matthew in the lineage of Jesus.[3]

Are there occasions when your indignation at the behaviour of others is, like Judah's, mere hypocrisy? Pray for the ability to see yourself as you truly are.

[1] Gen 44:18–34 [2] Ruth 4:12,18 [3] Matt 1:3

SUCCESS BRINGS DANGER

Think about an occasion when you were the victim of a false accusation. What emotions did you feel?

GENESIS 39

As Potiphar and the keeper of the prison entrust their affairs to Joseph, they benefit from God's blessing. No doubt they were impressed by Joseph's administrative skills and integrity. Yet, Joseph's success was due to God's presence. He has been badly treated by others, but God has not abandoned him and he himself remains committed to God. How easy it would have been for him simply to complain to God! What can I learn from Joseph's example?

But success brings its own dangers. Potiphar's wife is a woman who likes to have her own way. She is not prepared to take 'no' for an answer. Day after day she persistently pursues Joseph in order to satisfy her own lust. For her, adultery is no 'great wickedness' (v 9, NRSV).[1] She clearly has no respect for her husband. Perhaps she feels secure because she has the ability to manipulate him. Observe how she skilfully twists him around her little finger, as she implicates him in the affair by calling Joseph 'your slave' (v 19). If only her husband had not been so trusting of this foreign slave, she would not have been molested by him. Not surprisingly, perhaps, Potiphar unquestioningly yields to her.

Today's reading begins (v 3) and ends (v 23) by highlighting how God's presence with Joseph brings him success. As a source of blessing to others, Joseph is presented here as fulfilling in part the divine promises given to Abraham, Isaac and Jacob. God's blessing is always and only mediated through this unique family line. Indeed, later in the Joseph story many nations will come to Egypt during a time of famine and be indebted to Joseph for their survival. In this Joseph prefigures a 'greater Joseph' who brings God's blessing to all the nations of the earth.

Take encouragement from what this passage tells about God's care of us. Even when circumstances work against us, he works for us.

[1] This was a common Ancient Near Eastern term for adultery; cf Gen 20:9; Ps 51:4

NO DREAM ENDING

'Your word is a lamp to my feet and a light for my path.'[1] Praise God for
how he directs our lives.

GENESIS 40

Most dreams do not reveal the future. The dreams of the cupbearer
and baker, however, are different. What distinguishes them is that
they are paired together. The Joseph story contains three pairs of
dreams. His initial pair of dreams set in motion a sequence of events
that lead to him being incarcerated in an Egyptian jail. As we shall
see in tomorrow's reading, a third pair of dreams will lead to him
being released from prison. Since all three pairs of dreams originate
with God, he alone can give their true meaning. As Joseph readily
acknowledges, 'Do not interpretations belong to God?' (v 8).

What relief the king's cupbearer must have felt on being restored
to his official position within the royal court! This will have been
especially so when he witnessed the unfortunate fate of his colleague,
the chief baker. Yet we sense that here is a man who lacks true moral
character. Having experienced life as a prisoner, once set free he
immediately forgets about Joseph. There is no hint of gratitude for
what Joseph did. Nor, more importantly, is there any attempt to
investigate Joseph's claim that he was unjustly imprisoned. Enjoying
the status of his office, the chief cupbearer cares only about his own
well-being. As a follower of Jesus, how passionate am I to see justice
for all? Would I have remembered Joseph or merely thanked God for
being set free?

In the light of these dreams coming true, Joseph must have
wondered about the fulfilment of his earlier dreams. Would they yet
become a reality? No doubt he senses in these events the hand of
God. How disappointed he must have felt when the chief cupbearer
did nothing! Sometimes in the purposes of God, we need to persevere
patiently, especially when other people let us down.

**As you think on Joseph's role in this passage, pray for the witness of
Christians who come into contact with those who are in prison.**

1 Ps 119:105

A ROYAL SUMMONS

The gospel liberates us. Reflect on the life-giving freedom that Jesus Christ brings.

GENESIS 41:1–16

Two years of Joseph's life are passed over in a few words. It's hard to imagine how he must have felt during this long period, languishing in a foreign jail, for a crime he never committed, cut off from his family. Prison conditions cannot have been pleasant; jail was literally a pit (v 14) with no thought given to the personal hygiene of the inmates. Surviving in such conditions cannot have been easy. Not surprisingly, Joseph needed to be cleaned up before being brought into Pharaoh's presence.

If anyone had cause to be angry with God, surely Joseph had. Where was the God who had protected his great-grandfather, Abraham, when he was in Egypt? Why had God permitted Joseph to be treated so unjustly? Yet something sustained his faith through these difficult days of incarceration. Did he still believe that his royal dreams would be fulfilled? That would require extraordinary faith, given his circumstances. Nevertheless, Joseph appears to have retained a deep faith in God despite his desperate personal situation.

Pharaoh's pair of dreams provide the means by which Joseph will be released from prison. They underline God's foreknowledge of what has yet to happen. While for us the future will always be a mystery, God is fully aware of all that is going to occur. In the light of this, we should have a quiet confidence even when, as with Joseph, our present circumstances may seem exceptionally bleak. While our relationship with God is no guarantee that we will never suffer hardship, pain, or even death, we can face these things in the knowledge that something much better awaits us. For us, it will be a case of being cleaned up so that we may enter the presence of the King of kings.

Reflect on how your faith in God is affected when hardships come your way. Are you a fair-weather follower of Jesus?

GOOD, BAD AND UGLY

Reflect with thanksgiving on how God has guided you on your spiritual pilgrimage.

Dreams have a remarkable way of appearing very realistic. Yet, when we recall them, there is inevitably something very unnatural about what has occurred. What registered most with Pharaoh was the ugliness of the seven thin cows. As he retells his dream to Joseph, he expands upon what he had said previously (v 21). After consuming the seven fat cows, the seven thin cows remain thin and ugly. With good reason, the symbolic picture of what would befall Egypt was etched deeply on Pharaoh's mind. Unless he fully grasped the true horror of the seven years of famine, he might be lulled into a false sense of security by the seven years of plenty.

Joseph leaves Pharaoh in no doubt about the meaning of his dreams. Joseph's frequent references to God not only identify the source of the king's disturbing dreams, but also underline that God will indeed cause the seven years of plenty to be followed by seven years of famine. Given his own personal journey from favoured son to imprisoned slave, it is noteworthy that Joseph affirms very positively the sovereign power of God (vs 28,32). Later, Joseph will declare to his brothers that God was at work even in the harm that they intended to do him.[1]

Perceptively, the Egyptian king and his courtiers see Joseph as someone 'in whom is the spirit of God' (vs 37,38). Taking an exceptionally courageous step, Pharaoh appoints the young Hebrew slave over his royal house and the whole of Egypt. His decision, however, results in blessing for his people. Like Pharaoh, we too must trust our lives to a 'greater Joseph'. This also requires courage, as well as faith in the one we trust.

Look back over your own life and recall some of the events which now strike you as reflecting the providential activity of God. Thank God for his presence with you.

[1] Gen 50:20

RAGS TO RICHES

Take time to praise God for his faithfulness to you over the past days, weeks, months and years.

GENESIS 41:41–57

Joseph exchanged the squalor and filth of an Egyptian prison for the luxury and wealth of the royal court. Who could ever have imagined that Joseph would be transformed from an insignificant immigrant prisoner into the highly honoured prime minister of Egypt? Few rags-to-riches stories match this one. Yet this is not a rags-to-riches story based on human effort. Joseph does not work his way up the governmental ladder through personal endeavour. It is all of God. In a similar way, for every follower of Jesus, it is a rags-to-riches transformation. Like Joseph, we exchange our old clothes for new ones, being clothed in the righteousness of Christ. This too is all of God.

Some 13 years have passed since Joseph was sold by his brothers into slavery. As Joseph moves into his thirties, life is very different. God blesses him with two sons. In naming them, Joseph affirms that it is time to move on. The past is forgotten and his present fruitfulness celebrated. All of this is thanks to God. Joseph's God-centred approach to life has not been displaced by his new career. The one who made it possible for him to be prime minister continues to influence all that he does. We too should be thankful for the ability to forget the past and move on. This also is a gift from God.

In the providence of God, Joseph's life was transformed. From Joseph's perspective, things must have moved very slowly. Yet, in the end, his loyalty to God was fully rewarded. Sometimes in our impatience we want an instant fix for the challenges and difficulties that we face. In the light of Joseph's experience it is important to realise that God's timing may require us to wait patiently.[1]

We live in a world where everyone wants quick fixes to all their problems. Pray for patience to wait for God's answer in God's time.

[1] Ps 37:7–9; Rev 1:9; 14:12

THE SILENT MINORITY

Prayerfully ask God to speak to you in a meaningful way from his Word today.

GENESIS 42:1–24

About twenty years have passed since the brothers last saw Joseph, then a teenager. Famine in Canaan now forces them to travel to Egypt in search of food. When their journey brings them face to face with Joseph, his brothers do not recognise him. What reason would they have had to suspect that the Egyptian official before whom they bowed was their own flesh and blood? Naturally, however, Joseph recognises them and immediately recalls his earlier dreams. The very dreams that had previously caused his brothers to sell him into slavery in Egypt are now being realised.

Joseph, however, is reluctant to reveal his identity. At first sight his reaction may seem somewhat vindictive. He accuses them of being spies and imprisons them for three days. Is this a case of getting back at them? Possibly. Yet Joseph relents. He reverses his initial decision to keep nine of the brothers in prison, while one returns to Canaan for Benjamin. In the end he holds only one brother hostage. Moreover, by sending the brothers back with grain, Joseph displays generous compassion. How easy it would have been for him to do otherwise!

Twenty years may have passed, but Joseph's brothers are still haunted by their despicable treatment of their younger brother. Reuben, however, appears less than willing to accept any responsibility for what happened. His remarks (v 22) sound somewhat hollow. The initial account suggests that he was a willing accomplice, even if he did plan to rescue Joseph and return him to his father.[1] Yet over the years Reuben has remained silent. Now the 'silent minority' appears exceptionally hypocritical. Rather than own up to his own shortcomings, Reuben prefers to blame others. Are there times when I sound like Reuben?

Take time now to confess to God honestly and openly something which in the past you have wrongly blamed on others.

[1] Gen 37:21,22,29,30

THE PERSISTENCE OF GUILT

As you turn to God's Word, begin by taking a few minutes to confess to him those failings for which you feel guilty at present.

GENESIS 42:25–38

In the light of their earlier eagerness to sell Joseph for money, we might expect that the brothers would rejoice at finding the bundles of money in their sacks. On the contrary, they are filled with fear (vs 27,28). Sensing the hand of God in this, they are perturbed by what they cannot explain. A sense of foreboding falls upon them. Does their guilt about what they had done to Joseph colour their view of things? Do they feel that in the end their immoral actions will be punished? Our guilt for past actions cannot be easily assuaged. Only those who truly know the forgiveness of God can be completely guiltless.

Once more Reuben speaks up. His words give a clear insight into his heart. In the light of Jacob's concern for Benjamin, Reuben's offer (v 37) lacks both reassurance and sensitivity. A caring father would not readily put the lives of his own children in danger. Who would trust someone who was so willing to have his own sons put to death? Jacob was not impressed.

Reuben's willingness to pledge the lives of his two sons stands in sharp contrast to Jacob's stubborn refusal to let Benjamin go down to Egypt. Jacob knows all too well the grief and pain of having lost Joseph, and he rightly fears for Benjamin. Paternal love makes it exceptionally difficult for Jacob to contemplate sending away his youngest son. No father worthy of the name would uncaringly sacrifice the life of one of his sons. In the light of this, we can be certain that it was with great anguish that God the Father sent his Son to redeem us from death.[1] Had there been another way to restore the whole of creation, Christ would not have died on the cross.

Reflect afresh on what it cost God the Father to send his Son to be our Saviour. Give thanks to him for his generous, unmerited love.

---

[1] Rom 8:32

FAMILY IN CRISIS – AGAIN

'The LORD is my shepherd, I lack nothing.'[1] Thank God for his provision, even in times of crisis.

GENESIS 43

I heard recently of six children whose daily school lunches were placed on their kitchen bench in order of age. However, 11 adult brothers finding themselves seated according to age by an apparent stranger provides an astonishing end to a reluctant journey. Some time had passed since Jacob's sons' first visit to Egypt. The famine had continued; the food had run out. With his second son in custody and his youngest in jeopardy, Jacob had ignored his eldest brother Reuben's earlier offer to take responsibility for the safe return of Benjamin, but as the crisis worsened the third son, Judah, put himself on the line. He had disgraced the family name in recent times,[2] and may have been trying to make up for this. Or he may have been purely pragmatic: urgent action was needed to save the family, despite the risks.

The gifts taken to Joseph were the most precious available – agricultural products from Canaan and imported spices and myrrh. Silver, not native to Egypt, was valuable for barter; the double measure would compensate for the previous mix-up.[3] Due courtesy was paid to the trusted steward and Joseph, but neither paid much attention to the gifts. The overwhelming and culturally appropriate hospitality to the clan was their primary concern. The part humans play in this unfolding drama is complemented by the part God plays. Jacob's blessing of his sons as they left on their risky mission was that God Almighty – the God he had come to know and trust – would grant mercy and family protection in their endeavours. Joseph's steward indicated that their gifts were due to the favour of their God, and Joseph, in his private but overwhelming gratitude at seeing his younger brother again, offered a benediction. Their feast together was the first of much more of God's goodness yet to be revealed.

Give thanks for even small evidences of God at work in a family in crisis – maybe even your own.

[1] Ps 23:1 [2] Gen 38:13–26 [3] *IVP Bible Background Commentary*, p77

FAMILY SOLIDARITY TESTED

'He makes me lie down in green pastures, he leads me beside quiet waters, he refreshes my soul.'[1] Be refreshed in God's presence today.

GENESIS 44

Sometimes we hear of innocent people being tried for a serious offence. The prospect of a guilty verdict and consequent punishment is a fearful thing. Joseph contrives a second test for his unsuspecting brothers that will indicate how seriously they take the protection of their youngest brother and care for their ageing father. Will their innocence and fear in the face of accusation lead them to compromise their family solidarity to save their own skins? He has already accused them of being spies, and overheard their sense of guilt at betraying him so long ago – but is their regret genuine? He has observed their honesty in returning the silver planted in their sacks, and their determination to protect 'the boy', Benjamin (v 22), but are they just men intent on survival, or changed repentant people?

A prized cup hidden in the possession of his most favoured brother and an accusation of theft might just elicit the answers Joseph was looking for. The exact nature of the silver cup used 'for divination' (v 5) is unknown, but it was probably used for telling the future. Lecanomancy, reading patterns formed by pouring oil on water or interpreting omens in reflections on water, was common in the ancient world.[2] We know that Joseph sometimes gained his insight and wisdom about the future from dreams given and interpreted by God, but the ability to use these contemporary techniques might have reinforced his superior role under Pharaoh in the kingdom. Whatever the significance, the cup's disappearance was sufficient for a recall of the brothers to Joseph's presence. Their consistently humble and polite protestations verify a solid commitment to each other, and Judah's willingness to take the punishment in Benjamin's place sets the scene for authentic reconciliation. That true repentance has visible outcomes is a timeless principle.[3]

Do you face a situation that needs reconciliation in your family, work or church? Ask God for his peace and wisdom as you seek a way through.

[1] Ps 23:2,3a [2] *IVP Bible Background Commentary*, p78 [3] eg Zacchaeus (Luke 19:1–10); Peter (John 18:15–18,25–27; 21:15–19)

FAMILY REVEALED – AT LAST

'He guides me along the right paths for his name's sake.'[1] Are you on the right path?

TV 'reality shows' where family members are reunited are very popular – we love happy endings which seem to wipe away in an instant the hurts and loneliness of lost years. Imagine being one of Joseph's brothers as he tearfully revealed himself. Perhaps Reuben. Or Simeon, Judah, or Benjamin. Would you feel joy, knowing this man was your long-lost brother? Or anger at his testing and teasing? Would you question whether his story was really true? They were actually terrified just being with him.[2] Brother or not, they had double reason for alarm. Joseph, first rejected by them as a boy, was now revered as a powerful man who held the key to family survival.

However, Joseph's long explanatory speech was followed by hugs and weeping. The purposefulness of their dark history became clear – God was the designer of Joseph's elevation to political power. This saved not only the region from famine but their family line from extinction. Their short-term future as immigrants to the outlying Egyptian territory of Goshen was secure, and their prosperity was generously enhanced. Interestingly, from the historical perspective of family dynamics, Joseph showered his favourite brother with special gifts – maybe enough to precipitate another family squabble![3]

The best part of the story comes at the end – Jacob's unbelievable discovery that Joseph was actually alive after all. Again imagine yourself as one of the deceptive sons as they broke the news – how shameful it must have been! But Jacob's attention was not on this for now. His overwhelming delight is reminiscent of the returning prodigal's father – the lost is found! His stunned joy reflects that of the women at Jesus' empty tomb and the disciples in the upper room on resurrection day – Jesus is alive! His proactive faith inspires new hope – I will go and see him!

In the light of resurrection hope, ask (or thank) God for a surprising and re-energising outcome to a seemingly hopeless situation.

1 Ps 23:3b 2 *Cf* Gen 43:18,23 3 *Cf* Gen 37:1–11

FAMILY REUNITED – FINALLY

'Even though I walk through the darkest valley, I will fear no evil, for you are with me.'[1] Stop. Feel God walking beside you, lighting the way.

GENESIS 46

As Jacob headed south towards Egypt and reunion with his beloved son, he stopped at Beersheba, the last outpost of Canaan. This was no casual encampment; it was a deliberate pause at the place where he had grown up and his family had worshipped.[2] Its purpose was recommitment to the God who had brought his family into the land two generations earlier, and promised a nation, land and blessing to his grandfather Abraham through the line of his father Isaac.[3] Jacob's large itinerant family was evidence of the promise of descendants becoming fulfilled; the role Joseph was already playing in Egypt a foretaste of being 'blessed to be a blessing'. However, journeying to Egypt was problematic for possession of the land. Jacob had left and returned before, but this substantial move with his whole family in his old age was more concerning. So a special word from God to reinforce the promise of return was timely.

The Bible often records visions and encounters when God calls his people into new and challenging endeavours. Jacob's experience here preceded those of many well-known descendants, eg Moses, Isaiah, Mary, Paul. But this was not Jacob's first encounter with God. On his previous departure from Beersheba, escaping north to Haran, his angelic dream at Bethel reinforced the family covenant.[4] On his return home decades later he struggled with God beside a brook at Peniel, where pain was inflicted but blessing restored.[5] He had eventually settled near Bethel and established a new place for family worship.[6] This last recorded vision affirmed that it was the right thing for Jacob to join his son Joseph in Egypt, knowing that God's presence would go with him and his family. Joseph's welcome and his diplomatic wisdom on how to approach their new situation in a strange land made the never-to-be-hoped-for reunion complete.

Reflect on something God has promised you that has yet to be fulfilled, and wait on him expectantly.

[1] Ps 23:4a [2] Gen 26:23–33 [3] Gen 28:3,4 [4] Gen 28:13–15 [5] Gen 32:22–32 [6] Gen 35:1–7

FAMILY RESETTLED

'Your rod and your staff, they comfort me.'[1] Thank the Good Shepherd for his presence and guidance today.

GENESIS 47:1–12

Pharaoh was expecting the new arrivals. He and his officials were so appreciative of Joseph's contribution to their nation that they had generously assisted his family's journey and promised favoured status in Egypt. However, Joseph astutely suggested arrangements that would provide extra security for them. They were currently in favour, but in reality they were aliens – a different race, culture, language, religion, social class. They were a minority group with the potential to multiply rapidly. They were already quite prosperous, with the ability to acquire more wealth from their new context. Their stay was expected to be short-term, but we know what happened to their descendants when they were no longer in favour four centuries later.[2] So presenting a positive spin on the option of settling independently beyond the main hub of Egyptian life was to their advantage. Joseph's five unnamed brothers handled the negotiations successfully. They were granted permission to move to the north-western delta region[3] and inconspicuously continue their lowly role of shepherds.

Jacob's encounter with Pharaoh is brief and cryptic. We know much about his 'difficult' years: his conflicts at home and his enforced escape north; his years enduring trickery to gain his choice of wife and his own trickery in retaliation; his anxious flight back home to greet the brother he had cheated and his deliberate action to live far from him; his complicated paternity arrangements and bad behaviour of his children; and the loss of his favoured wife and favourite son. Even the joy of reunion with Joseph could not change the past. His interpretation of his years as 'few' was relative to the longevity of his father and grandfather who both outlived him by about forty years. The 17 years he was to live in Egypt brought some contentment.

Pray for refugees around the world. Displaced by famine, war or persecution, most don't have the protection Jacob's family experienced.

[1] Ps 23:4b [2] Exod 1:8–14 [3] Rameses was a name for the Goshen region – Exod 1:11

FAMILY SURVIVAL

'You prepare a table before me in the presence of my enemies.'[1] Rest awhile and enjoy God's hospitality and protection.

GENESIS 47:13–31

The recent global financial crisis made great demands of national and financial leaders throughout the world. We will not easily forget their anguish and panic as they rushed into strategies for curbing the crisis. Leaders have great responsibility for making tough, even unpopular, decisions in tough times. Joseph had managed the early stages of the famine crisis well, but as it became more severe the people's financial resources were not sufficient for the scarce, costly food. Creative leadership solutions were necessary to rescue the population. First came barter of livestock for food; then sale of land to Pharaoh with debt slavery of tenant farmers; then 20 per cent taxation of produce. Only the priests had special arrangements, probably an acknowledgement of their extensive political power.[2] Joseph's economic measures, which were probably enforced beyond his time, might sound harsh but they were humane in the context. The people had food and livelihoods and gratefully submitted to servitude to Pharaoh in exchange for their lives. Innocent victims of natural and man-made disasters around our world still require their leaders to resolve complex situations. Addressing contemporary poverty and environment issues with creativity, compassion and urgency will test even Joseph-like leadership.

We cannot speculate if Jacob's family should have returned to Canaan after surviving the crisis. Their material and numerical prosperity had significant early benefits, but in the longer term it nearly destroyed them.[3] The failing patriarch, however, was intent on going home. For Jacob, Egypt had been a welcome place for refuge and reunion, but it was not the land of promise where the ultimate security of his family lay.

Pray for national leaders who guide legislative, budget and programme decisions on behalf of those in crisis, both locally and globally.

[1] Ps 23:5a [2] *IVP Bible Background Commentary*, p79 [3] Exod 1:6–11

FAMILY SUCCESSION

'You anoint my head with oil; my cup overflows.'[1] Rejoice that, no matter what your human status, your heavenly Father considers you worthy of his never-ending care.

GENESIS 48

In many societies male firstborns are still favoured in inheritance, education and succession. This pattern was the norm in ancient cultures, so deviating from it is given special attention in the Abrahamic story. Isaac is chosen over firstborn Ishmael, Jacob over his older twin Esau, Joseph over his older brothers, and now his younger son over the elder. Family disharmony, deception and favouritism play a part, and we may cry, 'It's not fair!' But somehow God's plan for his chosen family – who themselves did not deserve it[2] – was not based on fairness but on God's sovereignty.

Joseph, recognising his father's impending death, took his two sons – now young adults[3] – for their farewells. The blessing was probably anticipated, but it took unexpected directions. First, Jacob adopted these two grandsons as his own sons – which explains the later inclusion of Manasseh and Ephraim as tribes of Israel, in effect giving Joseph a double inheritance. The passing remembrance of Rachel's burial is poignant, as she was the beloved grandmother of these boys she never lived to see. Then the birth order blessings were deliberately reversed, despite Joseph's protestations. Both sons were promised greatness, but later history indicates that Ephraim did indeed rise to superior influence and prominence. 'Ephraim' even sometimes became a synonym – sadly often pejorative – for the collective of tribes later forming the northern kingdom of Israel.[4] Joseph's name was not perpetuated in a tribe, but he was promised the ridge of land Jacob had bought in Shechem after his brief reunion with Esau.[5] It was nearly five hundred years before this literally came to pass,[6] as a key element of God's promise to the whole nation[7] to return them to their own land.

'We know that in all things God works for the good of those who love him, who have been called according to his purpose.'[8] Do we really?

---

[1] Ps 23:5b [2] Deut 7:7,8; 9:4–6 [3] Gen 41:50–52 [4] eg in Hosea [5] Gen 33:18,19 [6] Josh 24:32 [7] 'you' in v 21 is plural [8] Rom 8:28

FAMILY FORTUNES

'Surely your goodness and love will follow me all the days of my life.'[1]
Thank God for specific evidences of this in the past week.

GENESIS 49:1–28

Jacob now provides glimpses of future outcomes for all his sons. Eventually they would become tribes in the nation of Israel, each with its own territory in Canaan. There are many cultural allusions and historical portents, and wordplays and uncertain meanings are common.[2] We can consider only a few key elements. The sequence of sons is neither in birth order nor as in the pre-Egypt genealogy.[3] Here all six of Leah's sons come first, followed by the four sons of the two handmaids, then Rachel's two sons. Most of them would settle down and adjust positively to the challenges and possibilities of their new locations. However, the fortunes of some would be negative, even cursed: Reuben, Simeon and Levi would reap the rewards of their past immoral and violent behaviour.[4] Levi was the only son not to form a large geographically based tribe. However, the Levites' eventual role as priests indicated that their initial curse was turned into blessing as they eventually scattered to serve across the nation.[5]

Two sons were promised special prominence with long, image-rich speeches. Joseph's private blessing was supplemented by a public affirmation of the ongoing presence of Jacob's God and his superior position among his brothers. Judah likewise would command praise from his family, and also victory over his foes and the benefits of natural abundance. The territory of Judah would become home to the nation's capital city Jerusalem, the location of both the Temple and the monarchy. There is a strong prophetic hint that from Judah's line will emerge a ruler who will impact nations. King David and his royal offspring initially fulfilled this role, culminating in the eventual arrival of King Jesus – the triumphant Lion of the tribe of Judah.[6]

Imagine composing a blessing for your own children or future generations. What words of encouragement and insight might you offer?

[1] Ps 23:6a [2] TNIV footnotes; *IVP Bible Background Commentary*, p80 [3] Gen 29,30,35; 46:8–25 [4] 34:24–31; Gen 35:22 [5] Josh 13:14,33 [6] Rev 5:5

FAMILY IN MOURNING

'I will dwell in the house of the LORD for ever.'[1] Does this prospect bring you delight today? Or some other response?

GENESIS 49:29 – 50:14

With Jacob's individual blessings completed, and a final reminder of his specific burial arrangements expressed, his eventful life comes to an end. Those of us who have sat with dying parents will know something of the mixed feelings of his sons: gratitude for a precious relationship and sadness that it is over, combined with relief that frailty and pain are gone; then preparations for the final goodbye.

Joseph used his Egyptian networks to assist with the funeral formalities. Embalming, intended to preserve a body for life beyond death, was common in wealthier Egyptian circles. Internal organs were professionally removed, then the body soaked in special fluids for 40 days. In Israelite history only Jacob and Joseph were embalmed,[2] in preparation for their eventual burial in Canaan. Jacob was mourned not only by his immediate family but also for a lengthy period by the Egyptians, either as a sign of honour for Joseph's father or in his own right as a significant citizen. Even Pharaoh respected Jacob's burial wishes and his dignitaries supported the extended family in their journey and rituals. Their strong presence would ensure that the large company returned to Egypt, as would leaving the children and herds behind. It would be 400 years before the even larger family could leave Egypt for good, that time with opposition from the pharaoh.[3]

The long journey northward via trans-Jordan seems to have been completed in two stages: first with a week-long public mourning at Adad's threshing floor – an unidentifiable place of commerce near the Jordan, renamed in memory of the event; then a private burial in the more southerly family plot at Mamre near Hebron in Canaan.[4] Jacob was finally home with his ancestors, and the family retained a small stake in the future land of promise.

How would you like your death to be commemorated? What signs of hope would your family and friends celebrate?

[1] Ps 23:6b [2] Gen 50:26; *IVP Bible Background Commentary*, p81 [3] Exod 12:29–32; 14:5–8 [4] Gen 23:17–20; 25:7–10

FAMILY IN PERSPECTIVE

Reflect on your most treasured family friendship. What actions and attitudes help such a relationship to flourish? For some ideas, see Colossians 3:12–14.

GENESIS 50:15–26

Have you ever been afraid you might get into serious trouble if a person who usually stood up for you was not around? Maybe you were bullied, or had done something wrong. Jacob was now gone, and the brothers' fear that Joseph might take revenge for their earlier wrongs returned.[1] We have no record that Jacob instructed Joseph to forgive his brothers, but it seems that the reported request for forgiveness came from a genuine sorrow, not just from fear of retribution. It deeply affected Joseph, and prepared the way for genuine reconciliation. The brothers' prostrate gesture takes us back to the beginning of the story – Joseph's dreams came true, with a depth of meaning never understood in his youth.[2]

However, Joseph's willingness to forgive was only part of this story. Yes, he saved his family and many others in a time of crisis – but not merely by good management or good luck. Somehow the evil intentions of his brothers were turned around by the good intentions of the God who had already called their ancestors into a new, purposeful relationship. Joseph could only work alongside a saving God and offer his brothers kindly protection. Many centuries later – 'for such a time as this' – God placed a young Jewish girl in the courts of a foreign king to save her people.[3] And several centuries beyond that, Jesus came at the right time to offer salvation to the whole world.[4] Joseph's old age went well beyond typical Egyptian life expectancy.[5] His death rituals were Egyptian, but his hope was not: he looked forward to the time when he and his 'brother Israelites' would rejoin their ancestors in their own land. Inspired by his lifelong faith, he had no doubt God would make sure of that. He saw both his own life and his family's from God's perspective.

What faith perspectives guide your life – your decisions, actions, relationships, values, future?

[1] Gen 45:3–5 [2] Gen 37:1–11 [3] Esth 4:14 [4] John 17:1,2; Rom 5:6–8 [5] *IVP Bible Background Commentary*, p81

EXODUS

In Exodus, the dominant note is that of deliverance or redemption. It tells how God raised up Moses as a deliverer and then led his people out of slavery in Egypt.

On Mount Sinai, the special covenant between God and his people is established and laws are given to tell them how they are to live in relationship with himself and others. Elaborate instructions explain how he is to be worshipped, and the tabernacle symbolises God's presence among his people. After many years in the wilderness, God guides his people to the Promised Land.

Much of the Exodus story resonates with the New Testament. It speaks of salvation and freedom from slavery to sin. The Passover foreshadows the work of Christ, our 'Passover Lamb': '... we have confidence to enter the Most Holy Place by the blood of Jesus' (Hebrews 10:19).

Outline

1 Israel in Egypt	1:1–22
2 Moses the deliverer	2:1 – 4:31
3 Deliverance from slavery	5:1 – 18:27
4 Law and covenant	19:1 – 31:18
5 Failure and renewal	32:1 – 40:38

WHAT LIES AHEAD?

'Through all the changing scenes of life, / in trouble and in joy, / the praises of my God shall still / my heart and tongue employ.'[1]

EXODUS 1

Our reading starts with Jacob's descendants enjoying a prosperous life in Egypt. Did they expect this to continue, benefiting from the security of sympathetic rulers? Yet they were not where God intended them to be, in the land of promise. A change of dynasty brought dramatic reversal, with 'a brutalizing public policy that is ... all for reasons of state'.[2] Paradoxically, this was to be the path forward into God's purposes for his people.

The opening (vs 1-14) sets the scene for a story of two unexpected heroines, Shiprah and Puah, the first people named in the story of the Exodus. They were not afraid of Pharaoh because they 'feared God' (v 17), and God honoured them (vs 20,21). Humanly speaking, what could two midwives do against the might of a despotic Pharaoh and his officials? Much, when it is action trusting God! Today the media will be analysing the 'big picture' of events in the world – economic and political developments, climate change, ethnic and national conflicts, religious diversity, poverty and disease. These are contexts in which to exercise obedient, daring trust that follows the way of Christ and truly makes a difference. The midwives' actions are an encouragement for risk-taking individuals who call the bluff of today's pharaohs, who do not fear them because they fear God and see the bigger picture. Can you imagine the midwives laughing inside as they reply to Pharaoh (v 19)? Humour has a way of putting false, pretentious powers into perspective. The concluding verse of the psalm paraphrase quoted above is appropriate: 'Fear him, ye saints, and you will then / have nothing else to fear; / make you his service your delight; / your wants shall be his care.'

Are there difficult, even oppressive, situations in which God is calling you to act in fearless trust?

---

[1] N Tate and N Brady, based on Ps 34 [2] W Brueggemann, 'Exodus', *New Interpreter's Bible*, vol I, Abingdon, 1994, p697

CHOICES AND CHANGES

To the words, 'I will follow you wherever you go', Jesus replied, 'The Son of Man has nowhere to lay his head.'[1]

EXODUS 2

Life is full of choices as we respond to circumstances, but the consequences are often unexpected! Today's reading is replete with choices made by parents and daughter, by a daughter of Pharaoh and by the adult Moses. On the way, Moses' identity moves from being a Hebrew baby to an 'Egyptian', a member of the elite (vs 10,19), who nevertheless identifies with 'his own people' (v 11), and becomes 'a foreigner in a foreign land' (v 22). Choices are linked with who we see ourselves identifying with.

Pharaoh had decreed, 'Every Hebrew boy that is born you must throw into the Nile' (1:22), but the defiant actions of Moses' mother and sister resulted in the Nile becoming a place of deliverance (vs 3-10). Although having a privileged Egyptian status, Moses chooses to act on behalf of his powerless people[2] – but this results in him having to flee the country (vs 11-15). Like others before and after,[3] he becomes more than a spectator as he sits by a well where women come for water. Again he intervenes on the side of the powerless (vs 16-19) – and this leads to him marrying one of the priest's daughters. On the other side of Sinai, in a pastoral society, Moses finds a haven from the divisions, power and oppression of Egypt, but his personal unease is suggested in his son's name (v 22). He is to find that God has a task for him back in Egypt.

What diverse experiences are seen in this chapter: risky choices of parents and daughter, Moses' intervention identifying with oppressed kinsmen, and an apparently fortuitous meeting at a well. Our own experiences, like these, may seem disconnected, but looking back we may see how God is weaving them, with the choices we make, into the tapestry of life – often with surprising consequences!

Reflect on unexpected consequences from your past experiences, and on God's beautiful tapestry. Commit to him any choices you're facing at the moment.

[1] Luke 9:57,58 [2] Heb 11:24–27 [3] Gen 24:11; 29:2,9; John 4:6,7

THE ENABLING PRESENCE

'God has said, "Never will I leave you; never will I forsake you".'[1]

EXODUS 3

'I will be with you' (v 12). What phrase could be simpler? (It is only three words in Hebrew.) Yet can we ever plumb the depths of its meaning and implications? Moses met God and heard these words, not in a place of worship, but in going about his everyday work. When he asks God's name (expressing his character), the reply is enigmatic (v 14), with various possible translations for three words: the middle, 'who, what', and the first and last identical, '*ehyeh*, I am, I will be' – 'connoting continuing, unfinished action'.[2] The Greek translation (around 270 BC), 'I am the One who is', points to God as eternally present, reflected in Jesus' words, 'I am'.[3] The word *ehyeh* is also used in verse 12: 'I will be with you'. God calls us to follow him, and we come to know his character and desires ('name'): he will be what he shows himself to be. The God who journeyed with Moses' ancestors (v 6) is now acting in the dire situation of the Israelites – look at all the verbs with 'I' as subject in verses 7–10, and the first instance in the Old Testament of 'my people' (v 7). God would be with them through the deliverance and journey to Sinai (v 12).

Much later, when two people wanted to know something about Jesus, he replied, 'Come … and you will see'; his repeated call was, 'Follow me' and he chose disciples to 'be with him'.[4] The disciples thus came to see who Jesus was and what his name implied.

Moses' journey with God was not going to be easy (v 19), just as following Jesus involves 'taking up [our] cross'.[5] But Moses was not to be alone and nor are we. God is not a spectator urging us on, but present in the fray.

'I will be with you' – allow the words to soak into your whole being. Then go with heightened awareness and expectancy.

---

1 Heb 13:5 (Deut 31:6) 2 Durham, *Exodus*, p39 3 John 8:58 4 John 1:39,43; Matt 4:19; Mark 3:14 5 Mark 8:34

THE GOD WHO DIALOGUES

'Eternal God, creator of humankind and Lord of history, you have called us to follow Christ ... we feel ill-equipped and unprepared ... you promise your grace.'[1]

EXODUS 4:1-17

Moses is often described as the capable and courageous leader who brought the Israelites out of slavery. Our readings yesterday and today, however, suggest a deliberate purpose to show Moses' hesitancy and inadequacies! They emphasise that it is the Lord who is going to deliver, defeating Pharaoh, with Moses' role that of spokesperson, both to the Israelites and to Pharaoh – and even there he needed help. Similar stories, with much variation, are repeated throughout the history of God's people right through to today. The detailed dialogue can help us reflect on our tendency to focus on human resources, whether the abilities of others whom God has called or our own inabilities and excuses when we sense God calling us. The focusing drumbeat here is that the God who calls enables.

After years of a stable life, Moses at first is hesitant (3:11). Does he understand 'immediately and intuitively that this summons from the God of promise and liberation is a threat to his own life'?[2] God's answer is to promise his presence (3:12), expanding with all-embracing statements of what 'I' will do (3:15-22). Despite promises, Moses is afraid of rejection (v 1), to which God graciously answers with immediate signs, demonstrating his power (vs 3-9).[3] At Moses' claim of unsuitability (v 10) comes the reminder that it is the Creator who is calling and who enables (vs 11,12). Moses is still not convinced, so Aaron is introduced (vs 13,14). What an amazing cameo of God's call! Although the language shows increasing impatience, even anger, he does not compel or punish Moses. Rather the enabling presence of God who understands our strengths and weaknesses is seen as he meets Moses where he is by involving someone else alongside. Moses is still to be the spokesperson (vs 15,16).

Talk to God about your experience of his call at different times in your life and his enabling in weakness.

[1] T Falla, ed, *Be Our Freedom, Lord*, Openbook, 1994, p70 [2] Brueggemann, 'Exodus', p719 [3] *See also* Exod 7:8-12

FREE CHILDREN OF GOD

As children, we are 'heirs of God and co-heirs with Christ, if indeed we share in his sufferings in order that we may also share in his glory.'[1]

EXODUS 4:18–31

Moses' concern for his own people while he was in Midian (v 18), his meeting with Aaron (vs 27,28) and the believing response of Israelite leaders (vs 29-31) are straightforward steps on the path towards deliverance. However, in between come two sections that have caused much debate.

God 'hardening the heart' of Pharaoh (v 21) raises issues of human responsibility. Here, as in 7:3, God's action is in the future, but similar words later follow statements about Pharaoh hardening his own heart: 'the LORD hardened Pharaoh's heart' (9:12), comes after Pharaoh 'hardened his heart' (8:15,32). As previously in the call of Moses, the 'response of the humans who encounter YHWH, whether appropriate or inappropriate, often leads to a further response from YHWH which takes the human action into account'.[2] The words here assure Moses in the face of Pharaoh's future intransigence: Moses' words will be inadequate, but God's purposes will not be thwarted. Note the parallel: the continuation of Pharaoh's power, with the Israelites as mere property, is centred in his firstborn son, but God has wider purposes for his own 'firstborn son' (v 22), the one who receives the inheritance. Our thoughts go to the focusing of God's saving purposes in the Son of God. In Christ the powers that oppress have been defeated and all may enjoy the status and freedom of 'children of God', 'co-heirs with Christ'.[3] The second problematic incident is Moses' mysterious divine encounter (vs 24-26). This incident, with release through the 'blood' of a 'son', is one of the most enigmatic incidents in the Bible, but in some way, Moses, like Jacob,[4] is prepared for his task.

Straightforward events, the interplay of divine and human actions, troubling experiences – all play a part in the journey of faith.

In the midst of struggles and unresolved issues, encourage yourself and others with the knowledge that we are 'co-heirs with Christ'.

[1] Rom 8:17 [2] WA Ford, *God, Pharaoh and Moses*, Paternoster, 2006, p214
[3] Hos 11:1; Matt 2:14,15; John 1:12,13; Rom 8:17 [4] Gen 32:22–32

OBEDIENCE PROBLEMS!

'God of peace, let us your people know that at the heart of turbulence there is inner calm that comes from faith in you.'[1]

EXODUS 5:1–21

Have you ever acted in accord with what you believed to be God's will, only to find the situation made worse? How do you keep going, especially when colleagues criticise your actions and doubt your integrity? That was Moses' experience in going to Pharaoh. The clash is evident immediately: Moses tells of the Lord's desire for his people, for Pharaoh they are merely a labour force (vs 2,4); for Moses, the people are commanded by the Lord to 'hold a festival' to him and 'offer sacrifices', for Pharaoh he is the one to give orders (vs 1,3,4,6). Pharaoh disdainfully asks, 'Who is the Lord? I do not know the Lord' (v 2). Later the reason given for God's action will be that Israel, Pharaoh and the people should 'know that I am the Lord',[2] that 'there is no one like the Lord our God'.[3] Their future depends on how they respond to that knowledge.

For the present, however, Pharaoh lives with the delusion of power (vs 6-9). He ridicules their faith and makes greater demands to show who is in control (vs 17,18). The people blame Moses and Aaron who they see as having done wrong, so facing judgement from the Lord (vs 19-21).

We know how the situation is resolved, but what of our own experience when we are in the middle of apparent failure and others criticise? There is a time for re-examination: have we misunderstand what God requires or acted arrogantly? But there are occasions when our reading of Scripture provides clear guidance, along with the Spirit's inner conviction, and often the support of a trusted colleague (like Aaron). Sometimes a crisis is needed to bring necessary change. The lonely experience of Moses – and of Jesus and Paul[4] – provides encouragement to continue, leaving it to God to act to make known his reality.

Are you, or someone you know, facing a conflict situation? Pray for wisdom and perseverance, and that God's name be honoured.

[1] Falla, *Freedom*, p452 [2] Exod 6:7; 7:5,17 [3] Exod 8:10; 9:14 [4] Matt 16:21–23; John 6:66–71; 2 Tim 4:9–11

NO SHORT CUTS

'Now faith is the assurance of things hoped for, the conviction of things not seen.'[1]

EXODUS 5:22 – 6:27

'Rosa Parks sat so Martin Luther King could walk; King walked so Obama could run; Obama ran so we can all fly.' I wonder if you heard this saying at the time of Barack Obama's inauguration? It was deeply moving to see elderly African-Americans weep as they remembered their struggle and celebrated a new dimension of hope and freedom. Fifty-four years separate Rosa Parks' refusal to give up her bus seat for a white passenger in Alabama from the start of Obama's presidency.

At the heart of our text today is a sense of the suffering and deferred hopes that accompany every quest for authentic freedom. Moses confronts the distress and fury of the Israelite foremen and addresses his anguished protests to God (5:22,23), and the God who listens also responds. He invites Moses to imagine a not far distant future, 'Now you will see ...' (6:1), and to reconsider his understanding of the past (vs 2,3). Abraham, Isaac and Jacob had in fact known God as 'the LORD' (I AM, YHWH),[2] as well as by the name 'God Almighty' (El Shaddai).[3] They had seen God's promises fulfilled among their families. He had not done nothing (5:23) about his plans for his people. But God seems to imply (v 3) that the past generations had not experienced the full content of the name YHWH. This name 'is not a philosophical concept, but rather a historical one ... It testifies of one who is active in history, constantly intervening to realise a plan with the world in general and with a particular instrument, the people of Israel.'[4] Now, through a slowly unfolding process, Moses and his people will start to experience all the dimensions of God's name, beginning with liberation from slavery (v 6), moving on to a new identity – adoption into God's covenant people (v 7) – and culminating in homecoming (v 8).

How do you respond to a God whose plans for liberation seem so vulnerable (compare 4:30,31 with 6:9–12)?

---

1 Heb 11:1, NRSV **2** Gen 4:26; 13:4; 15:7 **3** Gen 17:1 **4** Falla, *Freedom*, p33

BATTLEFIELD OF THE HEART

'Search me, O God, and know my heart today; / ... See if there be some wicked way in me; / Cleanse me from every sin and set me free.'[1]

EXODUS 6:28 – 7:24

'The Bible is a dispute about the identity and character of the true God,' declares Walter Brueggemann.[2] The book of Exodus offers us demanding material about the nature of God. Pharaoh's question, 'Who is the LORD, that I should obey him...?' (5:2) may become our own question over the next few days (though in a different tone of voice). The atheist Richard Dawkins has written of 'the sheer strangeness of the Bible', the 'weird volume that religious zealots hold up to us as the inerrant source of our morals and rules for living'.[3] If we wish to answer him, we need to explore the difficulties of these texts with honesty.

The main stumbling block for any sensitive reader is God's declaration in 7:3, 'I will harden Pharaoh's heart'.[4] We have already heard this declaration in 4:21 and will hear it eight more times through the Exodus story (9:12; 10:1,20,27; 11:10; 14:4,8,17). We may note that there are also ten occasions when it is said or implied that Pharaoh himself is responsible for his obduracy (7:13,14,22; 8:15,19,32; 9:7,34,35; 13:15). At least in relationship to the first five disasters that fall on his people, it seems that Pharaoh's own wilfulness precedes any intervention by God. 'The battlefield of Pharaoh's heart is actually the central stage of the drama.'[5]

This will not satisfy all our unease, however. At the heart of the story is the mystery of God's activity, the God who delights when 'the wicked ... turn from their ways and live'[6] and whose longing to draw *all* his creation back into relationship with him is the storyline of Scripture. The plagues are not *punishments* on Pharaoh for his hard heart; they are repeated *opportunities* (especially in each aftermath; as in v 23) for a change of heart. What we cannot identify is the moment of Pharaoh's final opportunity for repentance.[7]

In the light of Romans 9:18 , pray for situations where a change of heart is urgently needed among those in power.

[1] JE Orr, 1936 [2] *A Social Reading of the OT*, Augsburg, 1994, p54 [3] R Dawkins, *The God Delusion*, Bantam, 2006, ch 6 [4] Cf Matt 27:3–10 [5] Falla, *Freedom*, p59 [6] Ezek 33:11 [7] Cf Rom 9:14–21

A WORD TO BE LIVED?

Thank God for the gift of imagination, and the ability to see familiar things from a fresh perspective.

EXODUS 7:25 – 8:32

'We are given this book so that we can imaginatively and believingly enter the world of the text and follow Jesus … There is no word of God that God does not intend to be lived by us.'[1] I find myself reflecting on these claims as I read this text today. Whatever could it mean to live today's word? How does it enable us to follow Jesus? If these chapters aren't somehow problematic for you, perhaps they've become too domesticated and familiar! Maybe you could try entering into today's reading, imagining yourself in the shoes of Moses, Aaron and their community, or Pharaoh, his elite and ordinary Egyptian families.

Through the centuries, people have responded in different ways to the questions about living this narrative. In AD 373 Gregory of Nazianzus explained a series of disasters in his community in terms of the Exodus plagues, and called all his people (without distinguishing 'righteous' or 'wicked') to repent. In recent years Kenyan and Zimbabwean critics of their own governments have compared their nations' problems to the plagues God allowed in order to set his people free. One Jewish commentator, Francine Prose, bravely stands in the shoes of the Egyptians and compares 'her childhood adoration of the plagues as recited in the Passover seder with her realisation as an adult that the plagues had human victims' (7:24; 8:18,20,22).[2] Dietrich Bonhoeffer advocated reading Scripture 'overagainst ourselves' rather than 'for ourselves' – that is, allowing the texts to reflect and interrogate us. Perhaps we begin to live this word when we ask if the communities we identify with (family, work, church, nation) are today more like the Egyptians or the Israelites.

Sometimes we can interpret Scripture 'in such a way that it supports rather than subverts corrupt and sinful practices'.[3] How can we try to avoid this?

[1] E Peterson, *Eat This Book*, Eerdmans, 2006, pp69,114 [2] SM Langston, *Exodus Through the Centuries*, Blackwell, 2006, p104 [3] E Fowl and LG Jones, *Reading in Communion*, SPCK, 1991, pp41,42

THE HUMILITY OF GOD

'Do you despise the riches of his kindness and forbearance and patience? Do you not realise that God's kindness is meant to lead you to repentance?'[1]

EXODUS 9

Richard Wurmbrand, the great Romanian Christian leader, wrote how at 27, dying in a sanatorium, he prayed for the first time in his life: 'God, I know that You do not exist. But if perchance You exist, which I deny – it is for You to reveal yourself to me; it is not my duty to seek You.'[2] God responded to his desperate prayer and redirected Wurmbrand's life.

If only Pharaoh had prayed similarly. He had twice asked Moses for pragmatic prayer on his behalf, to rid him of the discomfort of plague (8:8,28). Now some kind of turning point has been reached: for the first time since the start of the plagues we read that God 'hardened Pharaoh's heart' (v 12). Nevertheless God's humility and patience continue to characterise the story. I mentioned earlier the apparent vulnerability of the whole liberation enterprise, from its dependence on the ingenuity of the midwives and of Jochabed and Miriam, the involvement of Moses, that reluctant and insecure spokesman, to engagement with Pharoah. With nothing less than the rescue of his people at stake, why did God not intervene more 'efficiently' to secure his people's freedom?

But God's purpose of making his true nature, the full contents of the name YHWH, known, both to the Egyptians and to his people, must run its course (vs 16,29). He will continue to be patient. The devastating hailstorm (notice God's merciful timing, vs 31,32) will offer a further opportunity to Pharaoh and his people to recognise this God who has chosen to befriend their despised slaves, and to act on his word (vs 20,21). Pharaoh's first confession of convenience (v 27) is perhaps his point of no return (vs 30,34).

'People want grace, it seems ... But don't ask them to admit that it might take knowing oneself as a wretch to truly know grace for the wonder it is.'[3]

[1] Rom 2:4, NRSV [2] R Wurmbrand, *In God's Underground*, Hodder & Stoughton 1968, p15 [3] K Norris, *Amazing Grace: a Vocabulary of Faith*, Lion, 1998, p179

'SO THAT YOU MAY KNOW...'

Lord, help us to trust you to meet us and make yourself known, even in the most difficult episodes of your story.

EXODUS 10:1 – 11:10

'To suggest that God might intervene to protect us from the corporate folly of our practices is as unchristian and unbiblical as to suggest that he protects us from the results of our individual folly or sin ... our faith has always held that the inexhaustible love of God cannot compel justice or virtue; we are capable of doing immeasurable damage to ourselves as individuals, and it seems clear that we have the same terrible freedom as a human race.'[1] These words of Archbishop Rowan Williams in a lecture on Christians and climate change surely probe us as we enter with the Egyptian people into the horrors of locust invasion and the 'darkness that can be felt' (v 21) – probably caused by the hamsin desert wind. Today the 'corporate folly of our practices' relates not only to carelessness about our environment but to recent decades of cynical greed that have caused the massive global economic downturn that affects us all, but affects most severely the poorest people on earth.

If we are to read this text 'over against ourselves' we must surely at some point search our hearts to ask how we are responding, in the 'terrible freedom' that God has given us, to these world-encompassing crises. As we live through them, are we coming to know, in ways we have not experienced before, that YHWH is the Lord (10:2), and to respond to him? Or have we, like Pharaoh, become so practised in conditional obedience (vs 10,11) that we have now become the slaves (vs 20,27)? 'Every step on the way of sin leads humans further astray from the ethical choice they first had. One becomes more and more entangled in the net of evil.'[2]

'I serve a hard God ... / He thunders and kills / from below, in, above; / he consumes all dross. / He is stern / like love / and hard / like a cross.'[3]

---

[1] www.guardian.co.uk/commentisfree/belief/2009/mar/26/religion-anglicanism
[2] Falla, *Freedom*, pp57,58 [3] N Thomas, 'Hard God', *On the Edge of a Truth*, Barclay Press, 2008, pp104,105

BE ALERT!

Worship can sometimes become falsely soothing; it should prepare us for action.

EXODUS 12:1–20

The Passover meal is central for the faith of both Jews and Christians. It is the celebration, affirmation and reminder that we are a redeemed people. For Israel it is foundational for its self-understanding as a redeemed people, set apart as a priestly nation to be God's treasured possession, in order to reveal his character to the world.[1] For Christians it is also a sign of our deliverance from slavery to sin, celebrated as we participate in the body and blood of Christ in the Lord's Supper.[2] Sadly the biblical picture of Jesus as the Lamb of God is too often sentimentalised in Christian devotion as if he were a cuddly little lamb. A year-old ram is at the height of its virility and power, as such is not to be easily trifled with, and is roughly equivalent in age to a man of 30 years. As Dorothy L Sayers wrote, 'We have very efficiently pared the claws of the Lion of Judah, certified him "meek and mild", and recommended him as a fitting household pet for pale curates and pious old ladies'.[3]

The biblical significance of leaven is too often narrowed to be simply a picture of sin. Certainly it is that in some New Testament verses,[4] but it is equally a picture of the kingdom of God growing imperceptibly in an alien world.[5] Here, unleavened bread is a picture of the urgency of the preparation for departure, and the way in which it was to be eaten is redolent of the picture of the Christian as a soldier ready for action in Ephesians chapter 6.

Lord, may my armour be not just a Christian fashion accessory. May I be a good soldier of Jesus Christ, ready to march or fight.

---

[1] Exod 19:16 [2] Luke 22:15–20 [3] *Creed or Chaos?*, Methuen, 1947
[4] 1 Cor 5:6–8 [5] Matt 13:33

O LORD... AWESOME IN GLORY

Lord, may today's reading fill me with renewed thankfulness for the wonder of my salvation.

EXODUS 12:21–36

Much of the early part of today's reading is a recap. The Israelites, having found the favour of the Egyptians and been given many gifts, now create great fear among them. However, this does imply a change of mind. Whenever the people of God live up to their calling they often create this kind of paradoxical reaction of admiration/ fear amongst the surrounding populace. It happened in the young Jerusalem church after the Ananias/Sapphira judgement. Luke records various paradoxical reactions: no one else dared join them, though they were highly regarded by the people; nevertheless, more and more people believed in the Lord and were added to their number.[1]

Moses is aware that this deliverance was going to become one of the foundational experiences in the story of Israel's development. Israel's remembrance was not to become merely the remembrance of a past event but the reliving of the continuing experience of God's act of redemption. These words are used at every Passover celebration. In every generation one must see oneself as having personally come forth from Egypt, as it is written: 'And you shall tell your child on that day "This is done because of what the Lord did for me when I came forth from Egypt"'.

We need to look at our redemption in the same way. How do we answer the question in the old spiritual, Were you there when they crucified my Lord? Historically, of course, the answer is 'no – the death and resurrection of Jesus was a once-for-all event, 2,000 years ago'. But experientially the answer must be 'yes', for the crucifixion and resurrection of Jesus are not only once-for-all, but also timeless events in which we continue to share daily.[2]

'Tell out, my soul, the greatness of the Lord!'

[1] Acts 5:1–14 [2] Gal 2:20; Phil 3:10,11; Rev 13:8

A GOOD REPUTATION

Lord, may today's reading be an example and a challenge for my own life's journey.

EXODUS 12:37-51

As the Exodus journey begins we note that in spite of the urgency and danger of their departure, the people's concern is not totally turned in upon themselves. They take 'many other people' with them (v 38). No doubt some of these were the Egyptians who had been favourably disposed to the Israelites (v 36); others would have been some of those 'officials of Pharaoh who feared the word of the LORD' (9:20).

It was from the experience of slavery in Egypt that care for the stranger became central to Israelite spirituality.[1] In civil law they were to have equality with the native born Israelites.[2] But before they could enter fully into the life of worship and spiritual fellowship they would need to enter into covenant relationship with the God of Israel by taking upon themselves the covenant sign of circumcision. Here is a tension that we must work at also. We want to live in a country where all are equal before the law, where freedom to worship according to one's conscience is safeguarded. We want porous edges to our church membership so that all feel welcome and it is easy for people to come, to taste and see that the Lord is gracious.[3] But at the same time we need to guard sound doctrine, godly discipline and holy living amongst our membership. By remaining an open society, Israel frequently allowed itself to be led into strange beliefs and pagan practices and so came under the judgement of God. Yet it continued to keep its borders and society open to all in need. How can we work this out in our country, our society and our church?

'They are not of the world, even as I am not of it. Sanctify them by the truth; your word is truth. As you sent me into the world, I have sent them into the world.'[4]

---

[1] Exod 22:21; 23:9 [2] Lev 19:34 [3] Ps 34:8; 1 Pet 2:3 [4] John 17:16-18

CELEBRATING OUR SALVATION

May my salvation be a source of wonder and thanksgiving as I wake every day.

EXODUS 13:1–16

Before continuing with the dramatic narrative of the crossing of the Sea of Reeds, the author continues to discuss the future role that Passover would have in the life of Israel. Throughout their history this festival would continue to be foundational for Israel's self-understanding and would be developed to speak of God's redemptive activity in every area of the nation's history and prophetic future.[1] In the Synoptic Gospels Passover marks the foundation and climax of Jesus' ministry,[2] and in John's Gospel it is the calendar mark for some of the major points in Jesus' ministry, being mentioned ten times overall. Paul, in his pastoral ministry, uses the Passover theme as a picture of our holy separation unto the Lord.[3] And as we have already seen in the synoptic references, our celebration of Holy Communion and the whole Easter theme is directly linked into the Passover. Israel's deliverance from bondage in Egypt is a picture and a foretaste of our greater deliverance from bondage to sin.

In Jewish ritual, the Passover is seen as giving significance to the practice of laying tephillin, that is the wearing of leather boxes containing biblical texts, whilst praying, and of fixing Mezuzahs (small parchment scrolls, also containing biblical texts) to the doorframes of houses.[4] As Christians we of course have our own symbols, the cross being the most common. However, perhaps because it has become separated from actual biblical texts relating to it, it can become emptied of its meaning and be worn or displayed as just an ornament, by believer and unbeliever alike.

The remembrance of our salvation is one of the great motivations for our evangelism (1 Cor 11:26). How far is this true of me?

---

[1] 2 Chron 35:1; Ezek 45:21 [2] Luke 2:23,41; 22:1 [3] 1 Cor 5:7 [4] Deut 6:9; 11:20

THE ROUNDABOUT WAY

In what areas do you take short cuts? Take a few moments to think which are valuable and which, perhaps, are not.

EXODUS 13:17 – 14:9

Given that God has engineered the Israelites' release from Pharoah, it should be no surprise to discover he has also determined their route to the Promised Land. He has chosen for them the long road. They will not travel along the Mediterranean through the land of the Philistines, but 'the roundabout way of the wilderness towards the Red Sea' (vs 17,18, NRSV), south, along the west coast of the Sinai peninsula. Little did they realise that this was a journey which would take 40 years to complete.[1]

'The roundabout way of the wilderness' becomes a manifesto for the Exodus journey. Its purpose is for the people's safety (v 17), their spiritual growth[2] and God's glory (14:4). Knowing how they need reassurance and protection, God has provided a symbol of his constant presence and guidance. In front of their very eyes is a pillar of cloud each day and a pillar of fire each night. There is no short cut from slavery to freedom. It is as if these newborn people must learn to walk. They do not know the dangers; they do not realise their ignorance; they do comprehend God's glory. It seems that it takes at least a generation under the Lord's guidance to form the Israelites into his holy nation, who have learned sufficient about themselves and their Saviour to live by faith in the land of promise.

And so with us. The desert fathers (hermitic Christians following the tradition of Anthony of Egypt, from the fourth century onwards) chose to live in the wilderness so they could focus completely on spiritual growth and God's glory. Into what parts of the world's wilderness might God be urging you, led by the promised 'pillar' of his Holy Spirit?

Do you need a warning sign: 'God at work – please be patient'? Ask him to keep on forming you into the person he created you to be.

[1] *See* Deut 1:3 [2] Deut 8:2

GOD'S WORK OF SALVATION

'You did not choose me, but I chose you.'[1] Is this how you understand your salvation?

EXODUS 14:10–31

The crossing of the Red Sea provides, for Israel, the definitive understanding of God's deliverance in history. Rather than dwell on literal details of where the waters parted and how (the text does not aim to provide such historical details), the story invites us to understand some of the theological truths about salvation which are contained within it.

First of all, this salvation is entirely the result of God's initiative. God appeared to Moses at the burning bush 'out of the blue', asking him to rescue his people from Egypt (3:1–10). He was responding to a situation of oppression, but more fundamentally, he was continuing to bring about his promises through this people who had begun with Abraham.[2] Similarly, the birth of Jesus – God-made-man – was entirely an initiative of God, and a continuation of God's commitment to his people.

Secondly, the once-for-all delivering 'act' at the Red Sea is part of a longer story; embracing God's salvation is an ongoing process for the Israelites. The Red Sea act is the focal point and it is definitive; but it does not stand alone. The transformation of those who were saved at the Red Sea must follow, as we discover from the tales in the wilderness. The same is true of the life of discipleship and service that follows from embracing Christ's death and resurrection. Salvation is God's gift, but it demands our cooperation; and ultimately, our obedience. For Christians, the Exodus deliverance foreshadows the deliverance of Christ. Without it, we are resigned to 'slavery' and destined for 'drowning'. But in Christ, we are saved by God's initiative, and invited to respond with lives that recall and respond to God's amazing grace.

Spend time today simply praising and thanking God for his great act of salvation: for sending Christ into the world to die for you, before you were even born...

[1] John 15:16 [2] Gen 12:2,3

GLORY TO GOD ALONE!

'By grace you have been saved through faith … it is the gift of God – not the result of works, so that no one may boast.'[1]

EXODUS 15:1–21

Here is the song of praise and triumph which flows out of a people who have been rescued from death, the same refrain as sung by the apostle Paul centuries later. Exaltation breaks forth like a powerful flood, a jubilant song made up of variations on a single theme. There is no room for boasting about anything other than the Lord's gratuitous love for Israel. When the people are saved they lack even faith, not to mention deeds, upon which to build their hope. It is only after their rescue that we find it stated that they believed in the Lord (14:31).

Despite Israel's total victory over the Egyptians in military terms, there is not a hint of any self-righteous triumphalism. The introductory words set the tone for the whole hymn: 'I will sing to the LORD, for he has triumphed gloriously…' (NRSV). The words 'the LORD', 'God', 'he', 'you', 'your' reverberate from beginning to end and leave us with no doubt as to who the victorious champion is. It is his right hand, and not that of Moses, that has acted. Both the tragic destruction of the Egyptians and the role of Moses are downplayed – even ignored – while the power of the Lord is proclaimed with unabated intensity.

The song is not just about what has happened. It is also about the future. The passage begins with the words, 'Then Moses and the Israelites sang this song to the LORD', yet the structure of Hebrew language is not like that of English. The word translated 'sang' here has a sense that encompasses both past and future action. The liberation just experienced is not complete, as the song is not complete – yet. Now look up Revelation 15:3!

Use some verses of this song to praise God today. If you can commit some of it to memory so you can repeat it regularly, then do!

---

[1] Eph 2:8,9, NRSV

THE SCHOOL OF THE SOUL

'Guide me O thou great Jehovah … hold me with Thy powerful hand'.[1]
Sing this hymn in preparation for today's passage.

EXODUS 15:22 – 16:8

It has been said before, 'It is easier to take Israel out of Egypt than to take Egypt out of Israel'. The song of praise has barely finished before the people's cry turns to a murmuring complaint. Three days ago God held back the waters of the Red Sea; now, they are worried for shortage of water!

They take their concern to Moses (15:24) who takes it directly to God (15:25). God wastes no time responding – 'certainly, my dears' – and the bitter water is made sweet. What's more, God offers great reassurance of protection, as long as the Israelites are careful to listen to his voice and obey his commands (15:26). Indeed, the next place they stay is a five-star campground, overflowing with 12 springs (one for each tribe) and 70 palms (the number of fullness). For contemporary parallels, you may picture a swimming pool and a jacuzzi too! God provides his people with everything they need to follow him; indeed, more than they need.

Here, we discover how freedom is not a once-for-all event. It has to be learned, again and again. That is why Israel has to spend such a long time in the desert: it is a school for the soul. The redeemed people are still at the stage of my baby son, who, when he feels hungry, yells for milk with a piercing scream as if to alert the local social services – just in case his mother has forgotten him or abandoned him. He has no memory of the last time he was hungry, when milk was provided within a couple of minutes.

Where is your 'school of the soul' at the moment? Pray that you might learn its lessons deeply, so you may also embrace fully the freedom God gives.

---

1 William Williams, 1716–91

GRUMBLING AND GRACE

Are there things in your life about which you're prone to grumble? Look instead for the signs of God's grace.

The Israelites surely should have known better by now: that God is with them in the wilderness, guiding and providing for his people every step of the way. Yet they still look backwards, not forwards. Slavery has curbed their freedom of imagination as well as their freedom of movement, and they seem unable to conceive of God's love, his power and his generosity. It is so easy for us to look at the Israelites and see their stupidity and ingratitude – how dare they complain! But they are damaged people who need not only God's ongoing protection and provision, but also his patience and his healing grace. Meanwhile, God's reassures them with his continual presence – very literally – in the cloud right in front of their eyes (v 10).

There are some habits they need to unlearn. When God surrounds them with quail, and with bread – not with meagre supplies but with overwhelming quantities – their instinct is to grab it and store it away, in case it runs out tomorrow. Anyone who recalls wartime shortages in our own time might remember or still retain the impulse to do the same. God wants them to learn to rely on him daily: a very hard lesson for those who have suffered shortage, or experienced a betrayal of trust. It is helpful to consider the Sabbath command in the context of learning to trust. We can afford not to work – to rest – one day in seven because God is our provider and he is no one's debtor (v 29). The freedom to cease from our usual occupation is a sign of faith in a God who does not give according to what we deserve. Rather, he blesses us with more than we need.

Think: In what ways does God bless you with an over-abundance? Do you trust him enough not to hoard those gifts, but to share them?

TIRED OF TURNING TO GOD?

Does your faith grow tired? Ask God to renew you that you may 'soar on wings like eagles'.[1]

EXODUS 17

There are signs that Moses is growing weary. First, the people try his patience when, yet again, they complain about the lack of water. As his reply to them suggests (v 2), why do they turn to him and not ask God directly themselves? They should know by now that it is God who provides, and that he only needs to be asked. Notice that Moses also turns to God himself, but this time he brings his own personal concerns rather than praying for water on behalf of others. He is getting desperate.

There is not only the problem of internal unrest within the camp, but also the external threat of the Amalekites. Moses is absolutely clear that this battle, like those concerning water and food, is a matter of faith and trust. Thus he takes up his position on the hill, standing with God's staff (v 9), to pray. Holding his hands in the air – as we have seen him do so many times earlier (9:29; 10:12; 14:16) – is a symbol of his appeal to God for help.

Even Moses grows tired in prayer. (Does that make you feel better?) But he does not give up. Instead, he asks for help, and we are given the delightful image of two colleagues who stand on either side of him to prop up his hands, so that he can continue to pray (v 12). Here, 'eagles' wings' take a more down-to-earth practical form: sometimes simply asking for help is the answer to spiritual renewal. You might like to pause and draw a picture of this – even a simple diagram with 'stick' people' – if it helps the message to sink in.

Do you know where you need support? God's way of renewal may be through the practical help of a friend. Check that you are not too afraid or too proud to ask…

---

[1] Isa 40:31

MANAGEMENT CONSULTANCY

Are you in the habit of giving advice, or receiving it? Pray for the wisdom and humility to do both.

EXODUS 18

If 'delegation' was a buzz word in the management theory of the 1980s, then 'collaboration' performed the same role in the 1990s. Here we find the Old Testament offering the same wisdom. I wonder, how often does this management case study get the attention it deserves?

Here is a delightful account of 'in-law' relations. Moses and Jethro meet, man-to-man and heart-to-heart. They each listen to the other: first Moses recounts the glorious tales of God's deliverance of the Israelites in Egypt and in the wilderness. Jethro rejoices. Then, having observed Moses at work for a day, he offers some sage advice on leadership strategy. And Moses implements it. The message here is deceptively simple, but its implications hugely far-reaching. To begin with, it is hard to overestimate the historical and theological importance of Moses in the Old Testament: he is the key figure in Israel's story of salvation. Yet even he must learn to delegate; even he is susceptible to burnout; even he is to work collaboratively. And, as it turns out later in the Pentateuch, even he is not indispensable.[1]

As I read this account again, I'm impressed by the way Jethro offers this advice. Firstly, he spends a day in patient observation before making any comment. Secondly, he asks Moses to give his view of why he works this way before expressing an opinion (vs 14,17,18). Thirdly, he offers the advice carefully: consciously supporting Moses' best interests, and with careful suggestions for practical implementation. I'm also impressed by the way Moses responds. He is not proud or defensive: despite his unique role before God, he does not appear to resist the 'letting go'. Meanwhile, the waiting lists are reduced and the people go home satisfied (v 23)!

Ask God to whom might you be 'Jethro', offering careful advice about letting go. Then consider in what aspects you could be 'Moses', and hear the suggestion to let go of something yourself.

[1] Deut 31:1–8

ENCOUNTER WITH GOD!

Would you say there had been 'mountain-top' moments in your spiritual life? What features mark them out for you?

EXODUS 19

This is a momentous chapter in the Old Testament. Here, at Mount Sinai, God forges a new relationship with Israel – a covenant – to which Israel will ever look back to for its identity and security. This is the day God has been preparing the people for throughout the wilderness time since leaving Egypt.

The covenant is entirely God's initiative: he voices the invitation to Moses in verses 4 to 6, who subsequently presents it to the elders and the people (vs 7,8). On the basis of their experience of God's faithfulness so far ('You yourselves have seen … how I carried you …', v 4), they are invited to make a formal commitment in their relationship with God ('obey me fully and keep my covenant', v 5). As to the consequences, they will become God's uniquely precious people, distinct from all other peoples on earth (vs 5b,6).

The covenant is a two-way relationship: both God's commitment to Israel, and the expectation that they will respond with commitment in turn, are expressed here. The outcome of this relationship is also momentous: God has plans for this people which are universal in scope, as a kingdom of priests and a holy nation (v 6).[1] Here, the word 'holy' – which describes the Lord and his presence – is now applied to his people. There is a clear suggestion that Israel should imitate God and thus mediate his presence and his character in the world. How does this remind you of the 'new' covenant in Christ[2] I wonder? In fact it is not entirely new: it represents a development of God's original promise to Abraham of blessing ('all peoples on earth will be blessed through you'),[3] with which the story of Israel began.

Reflect: through Christ you are an inheritor of this covenant, called to bear God's presence and character in the world. How do you do this?

---

[1] 1 Pet 2:9 [2] Heb 8:6–13; Matt 5:14–16 [3] Gen 12:3; Gal 3:14,29

THE TEN COMMANDMENTS

'I have come not to abolish but to fulfil.'[1] Lord Jesus, teach me how this is so.

EXODUS 20

Today's reading may be ever so familiar, known to you from childhood, perhaps. In both Jewish and Christian tradition, these ten 'words' (as the Hebrew calls them) summarise the whole of the Old Testament law that follows in Exodus, Leviticus, Numbers and Deuteronomy. They are so important that they are found again in Deuteronomy, repeated almost word for word.[2] They have come to represent, for Christians, that part of the Jewish Law of which Jesus said no 'jot or ... tittle' will pass away.[3] They are the only laws which God spoke to the people directly (vs 1,18) – after that they asked Moses to mediate for them.

Consider the ten as a whole. First of all, there is an introduction which is too often ignored. Here is the motivation for keeping the Law: because I am the Lord your God, who has rescued you from slavery, therefore... (*see* vs 1,2; 3:13,14; 6:3). Notice how grace precedes Law. Because God has brought salvation to the Israelites by his prevenient grace, therefore he now asks Israel to live in such a way as to guard this freedom.

Of the Ten Commandments, notice that the first four relate to loving God, and that the succeeding six concern living with your neighbour. It is loving God that comes first – out of which, we may suppose, loving one another follows. Notice too that the commandments are not all negative, as so often supposed: the first five offer positive proposals for how to live well under God, and only the second five guard us as to what not to do.

Pray that you might recall God's gift of freedom by the way you live today, and that out of this love might flow a love for the people he has placed around you.

---

[1] Matt 5:17b, NRSV [2] Deut 5:1–22 [3] Matt 5:18, AV

SERVICE AND FREEDOM

Paul introduces himself to the Romans as 'a slave of Jesus Christ'.[1] Do you feel uncomfortable about applying that to yourself?

EXODUS 21:1–27

Many translations use the word 'slave' in this passage rather than 'servant'. Maybe your response to the Bible containing laws which allow slavery is one of horror. However, what is meant here is not slavery as practised in the Roman Empire, or in 19th-century North America. It was a form of bonded service, which arguably acted as a kind of social security system. These laws challenge us to think about the provision we make for the needy in our society today, and how we can prevent 'caring' institutions and traditions from becoming oppressive.

People who fell into serious poverty or debt, or were abandoned children, would sell themselves into servitude in return for food, clothing and housing. These laws curb the possible abuses of this institution, so that it remains essentially humanitarian in nature. People are not to be kidnapped and sold into servitude (v 16). The length of servitude is limited (v 2). A woman taken as a slave-wife, perhaps because her family could not provide a dowry, has her rights as a wife protected (vs 7–11). The slave is the owner's property (v 21), but their physical well-being is protected; they are not just chattels (vs 20,26,27). Given this context, verses 8 and 9 become slightly more understandable. This culture has not the modern emphasis on personal freedom over all else. For some, at least, the security of serving a kind master was preferable. Of course, the reality is that freedom is relative, as those who are enslaved to poverty or other ills know. It was because Paul knew what it was to be a 'slave of sin' that he was happy to be 'a slave of Jesus Christ'.[2]

Aid agencies tell us that slavery is a reality today, involving agricultural workers, 'sweatshop' labour, the sex industry. Find out about it, pray for them and support their action against it.

---

1 Rom 1:1, NIV – 'servant' is literally 'slave'. 2 *See* Rom 6:20–23